Street by Street

C000263295

YEOVIL
CREWKERNE, SHERBORNE

Barwick, Bradford Abbas, Ilchester, Marston Magna, Martock, Montacute, Poyntington, Sandford Orcas, Sparkford, Stoford, Stoke sub Hamdon, Thornford, Tintinhull, West Coker, Yeovilton, Yetminster

1st edition February 2003
© Automobile Association Developments Limited 2003

Ordnance Survey® This product includes map data licensed from Ordnance Survey® with the permission of the Controller of Her Majesty's Stationery Office. © Crown copyright 2003. All rights reserved. Licence No: 399221.

All rights reserved. No part of this publication may be reproduced, stored in a retrieval system, or transmitted in any form or by any means– electronic, mechanical, photocopying, recording or otherwise – unless the permission of the publisher has been given beforehand.

Published by AA Publishing (a trading name of Automobile Association Developments Limited, whose registered office is Millstream, Maidenhead Road, Windsor, Berkshire SL4 5GD. Registered number 1878835).

The Post Office is a registered trademark of Post Office Ltd. in the UK and other countries. Schools address data provided by Education Direct. One-way street data provided by:

Tele Atlas © Tele Atlas N.V.

Mapping produced by the Cartographic Department of The Automobile Association. A01554

A CIP Catalogue record for this book is available from the British Library.
Printed by GRAFIASA S.A., Porto, Portugal
The contents of this atlas are believed to be correct at the time of the latest revision. However, the publishers cannot be held responsible for loss occasioned by any person acting or refraining from action as a result of any material in this atlas, nor for any errors, omissions or changes in such material. This does not affect your statutory rights. The publishers would welcome information to correct any errors or omissions and to keep this atlas up to date. Please write to Publishing, The Automobile Association, Fanum House (FH17), Basing View, Basingstoke, Hampshire, RG21 4EA.

Ref: ML139

Key to map pages	ii-iii
Key to map symbols	iv-1
Enlarged scale pages	2-3
Street by Street	4-51
Index – towns & villages	52
Index – streets	53-56
Index – featured places	56-57

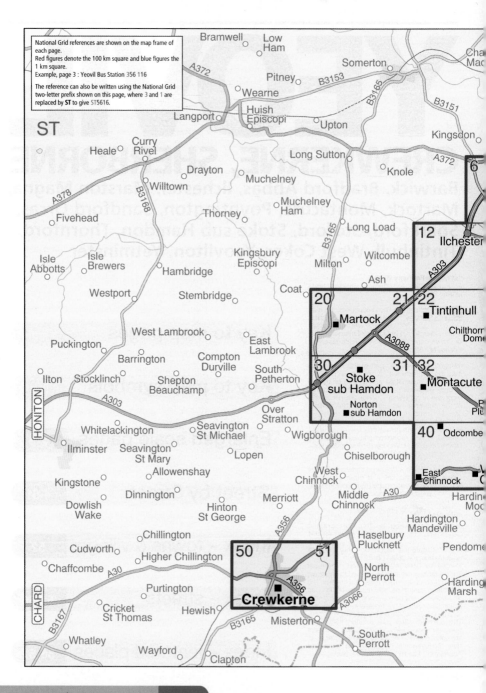

ii

ST

National Grid references are shown on the map frame of each page.
Red figures denote the 100 km square and blue figures the 1 km square.
Example, page 3 : Yeovil Bus Station 356 116

The reference can also be written using the National Grid two-letter prefix shown on this page, where 3 and 1 are replaced by **ST** to give ST5616.

Bramwell
Low Ham
Somerton
A372
B3153
Pitney
B3165
Wearne
B3151
Huish Episcopi
Langport
Upton
Kingsdon
Heale
Curry Rivel
Long Sutton
A372
Drayton
Knole
6
Willtown
Muchelney
12
Fivehead
Muchelney Ham
Ilchester
Thorney
Long Load
Isle Abbotts
Isle Brewers
Kingsbury Episcopi
Witcombe
A303
Hambridge
Milton
Ash
Westport
Stembridge
Coat
20
21 22
Tintinhull
West Lambrook
Martock
Chilthorn Dome
Puckington
East Lambrook
A3088
Barrington
Compton Durville
30
31 32
Ilton
Stocklinch
Shepton Beauchamp
South Petherton
Stoke sub Hamdon
Montacute
A303
Norton sub Hamdon
HONITON
Over Stratton
40
Odcombe
Whitelackington
Seavington St Michael
Wigborough
Ilminster
Seavington St Mary
Lopen
Chiselborough
Allowenshay
West Chinnock
East Chinnock
Kingstone
Middle Chinnock
A30
Harding Moo
Dinnington
Merriott
Dowlish Wake
Hinton St George
Hardington Mandeville
Chillington
Haselbury Plucknett
Pendome
Cudworth
Higher Chillington
50
51
North Perrott
Harding Marsh
Chaffcombe
A30
Purtington
Crewkerne
A356
A3066
CHARD
Cricket St Thomas
Hewish
Misterton
South Perrott
B3167
Whatley
Wayford
Clapton
B3165

A372
A378
B3168
B3165

Enlarged scale pages   1:10,000   6.3 inches to 1 mile

0 ————————— 1/4 ————————— miles ————————— 1/2
0 ———— 1/4 ———— 1/2 ———— kilometres ———— 3/4 ———— 1

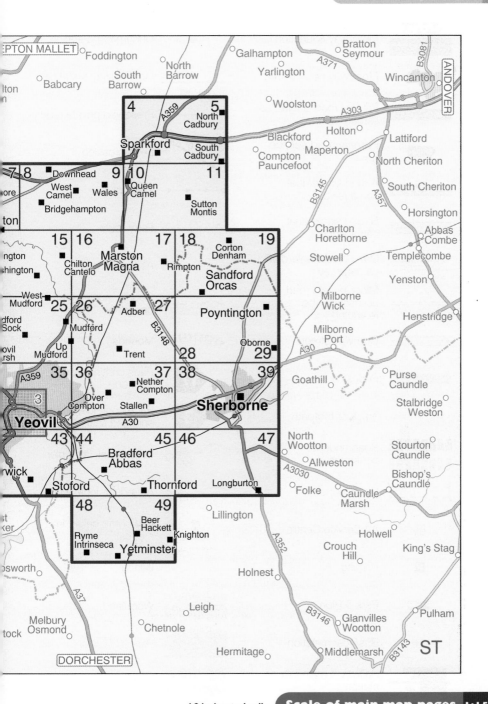

EPTON MALLET Foddington
North Barrow
Galhampton
Bratton Seymour
A371
Wincanton
B3081
ANDOVER

Iton
n
Babcary
South Barrow
Yarlington
Woolston
A303
Andover

4
North Cadbury
5
A359
Blackford
Holton
Maperton
Lattiford

Sparkford
South Cadbury
Compton Pauncefoot
North Cheriton
B3145
South Cheriton
A357
Horsington

7 8 Downhead 9 10 11
West Camel
Wales
Queen Camel
Sutton Montis
Abbas Combe
Templecombe
Yenston

ore
ton
Bridgehampton

15 16 17 18 19
Charlton Horethorne
Stowell
Henstridge

ngton
shington
Chilton Cantelo
Marston Magna
Rimpton
Corton Denham
Sandford Orcas
Milborne Wick

West Mudford
25 26 27
Adber
Poyntington
Milborne Port
A30
Goathill

dford Sock
ovil rsh
Mudford
Up Mudford
Trent
28
Oborne
29
Purse Caundle

A359
35 36 37 38 39
Nether Compton
Over Compton
Stallen
Sherborne
Goathill
Stalbridge Weston

3
Yeovil
A30

43 44 45 46 47
Bradford Abbas
North Wootton
Allweston
Stourton Caundle
Bishop's Caundle

wick
Stoford
Thornford
Longburton
A3030
Folke
Caundle Marsh

48 49
Beer Hackett
Ryme Intrinseca
Knighton
Yetminster
Lillington
Holwell
Crouch Hill
King's Stag

sworth
A37
Holnest

Melbury Osmond
tock
Chetnole
Leigh
B3146
Glanvilles Wootton
Pulham
B3143
ST

DORCHESTER
Hermitage
Middlemarsh

4.2 inches to 1 mile **Scale of main map pages** **1:15,000**

0   1/4   miles 1/2   3/4   1
0   1/4 1/2 kilometres 3/4   1   1 1/4   1 1/2

iv

Junction 9	Motorway & junction
Services	Motorway service area
	Primary road single/dual carriageway
Services	Primary road service area
	A road single/dual carriageway
	B road single/dual carriageway
	Other road single/dual carriageway
	Minor/private road, access may be restricted
← ←	One-way street
	Pedestrian area
	Track or footpath
	Road under construction
	Road tunnel
AA	AA Service Centre
P	Parking
P+	Park & Ride
	Bus/coach station
	Railway & main railway station
	Railway & minor railway station

	Underground station
	Light railway & station
++++++	Preserved private railway
LC	Level crossing
•—•—•—•	Tramway
----------	Ferry route
....	Airport runway
—·—·—·—	County, administrative boundary
▾▾▾▾▾▾▾▾	Mounds
17	Page continuation 1:15,000
3	Page continuation to enlarged scale 1:10,000
	River/canal, lake, pier
	Aqueduct, lock, weir
465 ▲ Winter Hill	Peak (with height in metres)
	Beach
	Woodland
	Park
	Cemetery
	Built-up area

	Featured building		Abbey, cathedral or priory
	City wall		Castle
A&E	Hospital with 24-hour A&E department		Historic house or building
PO	Post Office	Wakehurst Place NT	National Trust property
	Public library	M	Museum or art gallery
i	Tourist Information Centre		Roman antiquity
	Petrol station Major suppliers only		Ancient site, battlefield or monument
†	Church/chapel		Industrial interest
	Public toilets		Garden
	Toilet with disabled facilities		Arboretum
PH	Public house AA recommended		Farm or animal centre
	Restaurant AA inspected		Zoological or wildlife collection
	Theatre or performing arts centre		Bird collection
	Cinema		Nature reserve
	Golf course	V	Visitor or heritage centre
▲	Camping AA inspected		Country park
	Caravan Site AA inspected		Cave
	Camping & caravan site AA inspected		Windmill
	Theme park		Distillery, brewery or vineyard

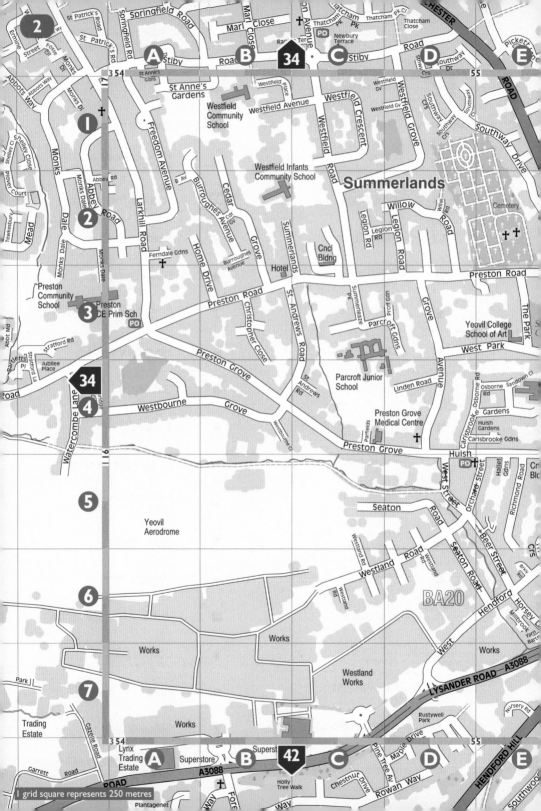

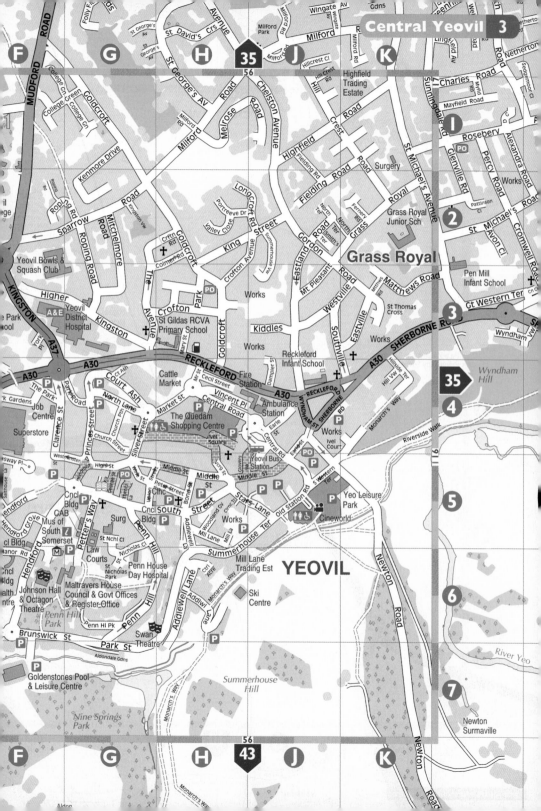

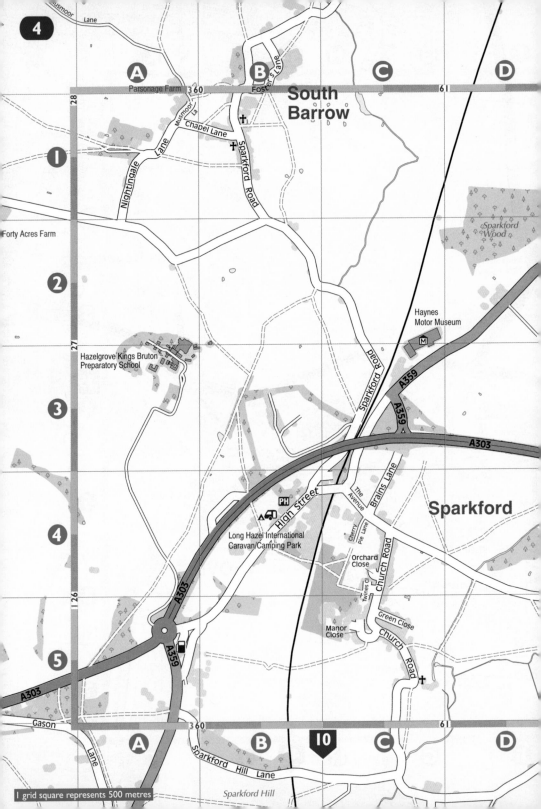

4

A   B   C   D

Musmoor Lane

Parsonage Farm   3 60   Foster's Lane   6 1

South Barrow

28

Chapel Lane

Musmoor La

Nightingale Lane

Sparkford Road

1

Sparkford Wood

Forty Acres Farm

2

27

Haynes Motor Museum

M

Hazelgrove Kings Bruton Preparatory School

3

Sparkford Road

A359

A359

A359

A303

Sparkford

Brains Lane

The Avenue

4

PH

High Street

Long Hazel International Caravan/Camping Park

Cherry Pie Lane

Church Road

Orchard Close

Twines Cl

Green Close

Manor Close

Church Road

26

A303

A359

5

A303

Gason Lane

3 60

Sparkford Hill Lane

10

6 1

A   B   C   D

Sparkford Hill

I grid square represents 500 metres

6

Kingsdon

Special School

Lod

Brinch Hill

Brincl Hill

Park Brook

r Road

B3151

A **B** **C** **D**

3 52 53

A372

Red Post Cross

EDMOND'S HILL

1

25

BONDIP HILL B3151

2

A303

3

24

Blackthorne Close

Little Meadow

Briarfield Millfield

Ilchester Community School (Junior)

Dragonfly Cl.

Chase

4

South Mead Farm

Taranto Hill

Channel Dash Pl

Illstrs Crs

School

Esmonde Drive

Central Av

A303

Hermes Pl

Eagle Cl

B3151

Great Orch.

Costello Ditch

COSTELLO HILL B3151

5

123

Northover †

Bl

A **B** **[13]** **C** **D**

3 52 53

B3151

Ilchester

Priory Cl

Lane

Works

Chns

Road

ca

Frrs Cl

MARK

PO

Town Hall

Ivel Gdns

Back La

Leland Trail & Monarch's Way

PH

Pill Bridge

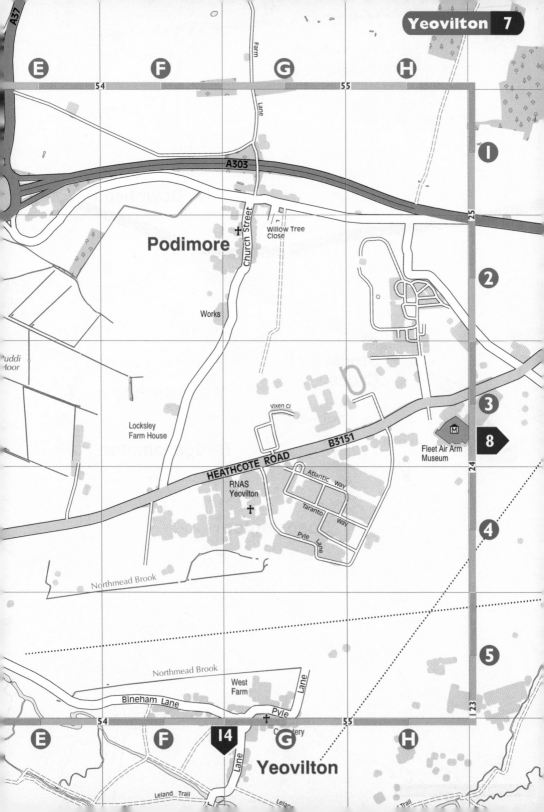

E F G H

54 55

I

A37

A303

Podimore

Church Street

Willow Tree
Close

2

Works

Farm

Lane

25

3

uddi
Moor

Locksley
Farm House

Vixen Cl

Fleet Air Arm
Museum

8

HEATHCOTE ROAD B3151

Atlantic Way

24

RNAS
Yeovilton

Taranto Way

Pyle Lane

4

Northmead Brook

5

Northmead Brook

West
Farm

Lane

1 23

Bineham Lane

Pyle

E F G H

54 55

14

Cemetery

Yeovilton

Lane

Leland Trail

Leland Trail

Parson's
Steeple

E   F   G   H
303
Gason

58   59

I

Canegore
Corner

Howell Hill

Lane

Traits Lane

Wales

Countess Gytha
Primary School

Blackwell   Road

A359

Church Pth

Gra

Leland Trail

Works

Church Path

England's Md   England's Lane

River Cam

Wales Lane

Church Pth

Church Pth

Green La

Milfamay Dr

Orchard

Mildmay Dr

Leland Trail

West Camel
Farm

Queen
Camel

The Glebe

The Glebe

Surg

Cleaveside Cl

Rectory Farm

Queen Ca
Health Ce

West
Camel

Parsonage Road

West Camel Road   West Camel Road

Rectory Farm
Close

2

CH   STREET

3   Camel
Farm

10

24

Spring
Farm

Lambrook
Farm

4

CAMEL

STREET

5

123

58   59

E   F   16   G   H

A359

Little

Woollen Lane

Marston

10

A303

A359

Gason

360

A

B

4

C

61

D

Church Road

✝

Sparkford Hill Lane

Sparkford Hill

I

River Cam

Road

25

Countess Gytha Primary School

Church ✝

Pth

Laurel La

Englands La Lane

Grace Martin's La

Rectory Lane

✝

West
Bamp

Englands Md

Green La

Works

Aldmay Dr

2

PO Surg

A359 HIGH

Mildmay Dr

Orchard

Leland Trail

Queen Camel

The Glebe

Cleaveside Cl

Rectory Farm Close

Queen Camel Health Cen

Leland Trail

Road

STREET

3

Camel Farm

Blindwell Lane

9

24

Windsor Farm

4

STREET

Lambrook Farm

CAMEL

5

123

360

A

B

17

C

61

D

A359

Woollen Lane

1 grid square represents 500 metres

Little Weston

South Cadbury

East End

Folly Lane

Compton Road

E

F

5

G

H

62

63

25

Leland Trail

Castle Lane

Crangs Lane

Cadbury Castle •

I

2

Henshall Brook

Church Hill

Allotment Road

Sutton Montis

Rectory Hl

Leland Trail

Buckland

Stonehill

3

Charwel Field

24

Lane

Kember's Hill

Kember's Hill

Sutton Farm

Whitcombe Farm Lane

4

Whitcombe

Monarch's Way & Macmillan Way

Girt

Beacon Lane

The Beacon

5

123

E

F

18

G

H

62

63

Ridge Lane

Ridge Lane

E F **6** G H

Northover

Ilchester

B3151

Priory Cl

Works

Pill Bridge Lane

Abbotts Road

Priory Road

Bshps

Cnns

Frrs Cl

Wk

Ga

PO

Town Hall

High St

West Street

Pill Bridge Lane

The Paddocks

Manor Cons

Almshse La

A37

Ilchester Mead

Back La

Ivel Gdns

Surg

PH

Kingshams

Freestone

St

MARKET PLACE

CHURCH ST

Lyster Cl

Limington Road

Leland Trail & Monarch's Way

Cemetery

Almshouse Lane

I

Mill Lane

Movey Lane

Duck

2

22

Leland Trail & Monarch's Way

Bearley Brook

's Way

Elborough Lane (Track)

3

14

4

Elborough Lane (Track)

21

Oakley Brook

Higher Oakley Farm

A37

5

BA22

E F **23** G H

Rushley Farm

Oakle Farm

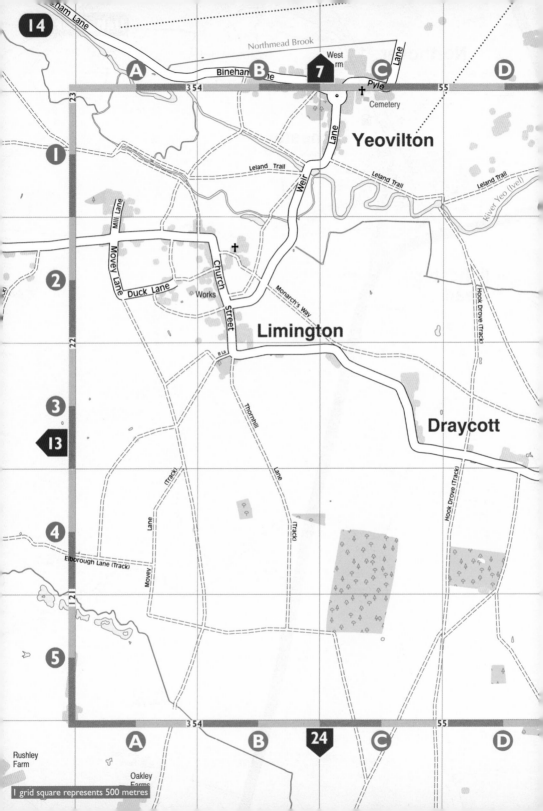

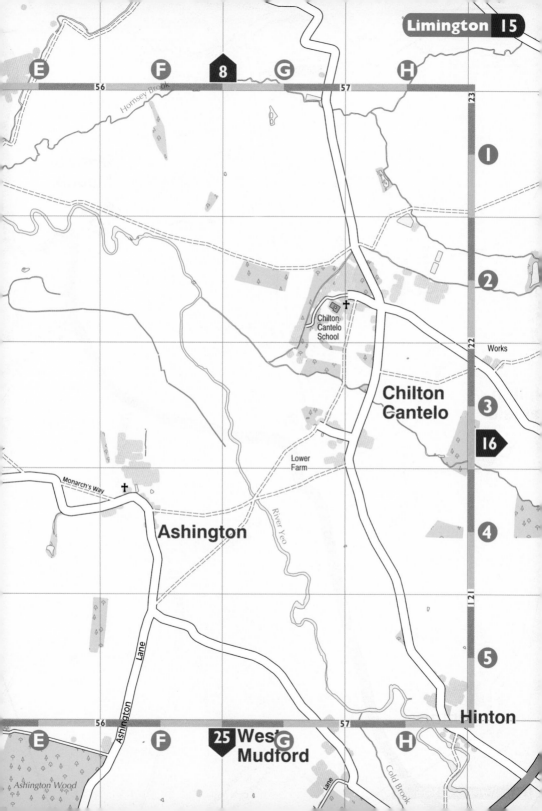

Limington **15**

E   F   **8**   G   H

I

2

Works

Chilton
Cantelo
School

Chilton
Cantelo

3

16

Lower
Farm

4

Monarch's Way

Ashington

River Yeo

5

Hinton

E   F   **25** **West**   G   H
              Mudford

Ashington Wood

Ashington Lane

Cold Brook

Hornsey Brook

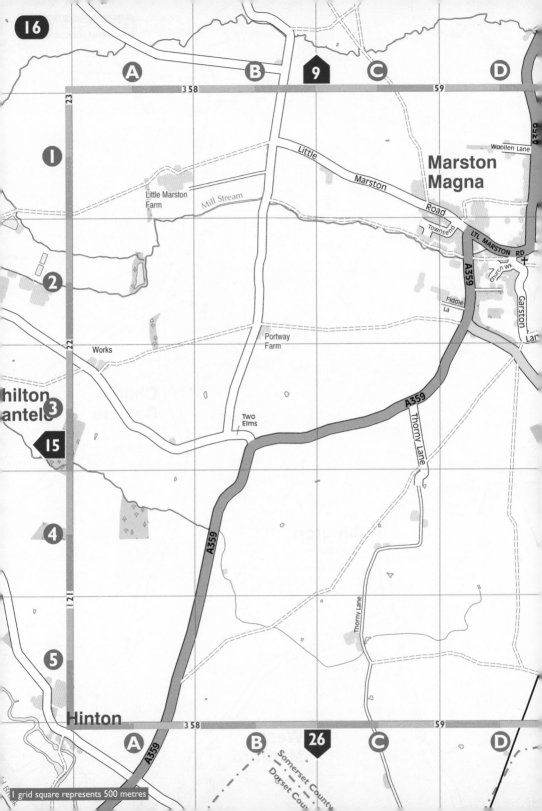

16

A   **358**   B   **9**   C   **59**   D

1

23

Little

Marston Magna

Woollen Lane

Little Marston Farm

Mill Stream

Marston

Road

Townsend

LTL MARSTON RD

Church Wk

2

22

Works

Portway Farm

Fiddle La

A359

Garston Lan

hilton antele

3

A359

Thorny Lane

15

Two Elms

4

21

A359

Thorny Lane

5

Hinton

A   **358**   B   **26**   C   **59**   D

A359

Somerset County
Dorset Cou

I grid square represents 500 metres

E   F   **10**   G   H

60   61   **23**

I

Road

mpton

Works

Netherton Lane

Woodhouse   Lane   Woodhouse Lane

2

rt

ens

Mill Street

22

Home Farm Lane

Middle Street

Back Lane

High Street

Church Lane

Parkway

3

18

Rimpton

B3148

Roe Lane

Roe   Lane

4

Heaven's Door

121

Slade Lane

RIMPTON HILL

Pitfield Corner

White Post

Great Pit Lane

5

E   F   **27**   G   H

60   B3148   61

dber

Great Pit Lane

Road

Field Lane

anmore

18

A   B   **11**   C   D

3 62   63

23

1

Ridge   Lane   Ridge Lane

Woodhouse

Woodhouse Lane

Woodhouse Lane

Woodhouse Lane

Cemetery ✝

Ridge Lane

Middle Ridge

2

22

Putts L

Weathergrove Farm

Pink Knoll Hollow

3

17

Windmill Hill

Monarch's Way & Macmillan Wy

Monarch's Way & Macmillan Way

Stafford Green

Roe Lane

4

21

Winter Lane

Monarch's Way

5

Great Pit Lane

Dark Lane

Shiller's Lane

✝

Sandford Orcas   **28**

A   B   C   D

3 62   63

Road

Lane

H

Higher

1 grid square represents 500 metres

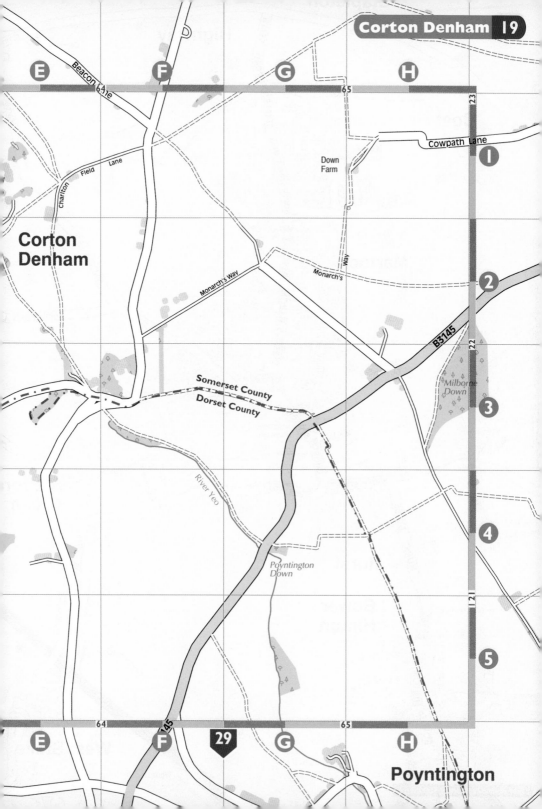

E
F
G
H

Beacon Gate

65

23

Cowpath Lane

I

Down
Farm

Charlton Field Lane

**Corton
Denham**

Monarch's Way

Monarch's Way

Monarch's

2

B3145

22

Milborne
Down

3

Somerset County

Dorset County

River Yeo

4

21

Poyntington
Down

5

64

3145

29

65

E
F
G
H

Poyntington

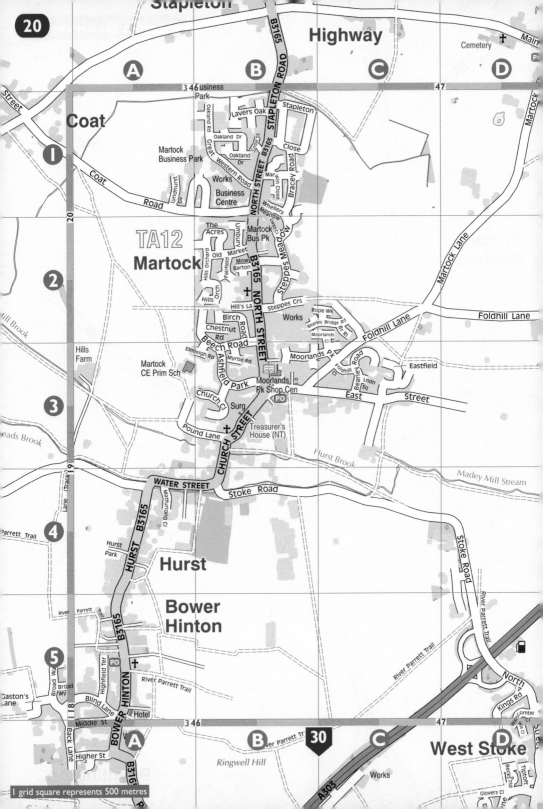

Stapleton

Highway

Cemetery

Street

Coat

A   B   C   D

3 46 usiness Park

47

Lavers Oak

Stapleton

B3165

STAPLETON ROAD

1

Martock Business Park

Coat Road

Oakland Rd

Great Western Road

Oakland Dr

Oakland Dr

Lynhurst Gv

Works

Business Centre

NORTH STREET

B3165

Close

Bracey Road

Marsh Close

Wheelers Meadow

20

TA12

Martock

The Acres

Limbury

Martock Bus Pk

Old Market

Steppes Meadow

2

Hills Orchard

Fairfield

Mow Barton

B3165

NORTH STREET

Hills Orch

Hill's La

Steppes Crs

Foldhill Lane

Hills

Birch Road

Works

Rope Wk

Bearley Bridge Rd

Bridge Rd

Foldhill Lane

Hills Farm

Chestnut Rd

Beech Road

Moorlands

Cl

Foldhill Road

Eastfield

Martock CE Prim Sch

Elmleigh Rd

Ashfield Park

Myrtle Rd

Moorlands Pk

Bearley Road

Lndn Sq

3

Church C

Surg

Moorlands Pk Shop Cen

PO

Foldhill Cl

East Street

Pound Lane

CHURCH STREET

Treasurer's House (NT)

Hurst Brook

Madey Mill Stream

eads Brook

Lane (Track)

19

WATER STREET

Stoke Road

Mathurlong Cl

4

Hurst Park

HURST B3165

Hurst

Stoke Road

River Parrett Trail

Bower Hinton

River Parrett Trail

River Parrett Trail

5

Gaston's Lane

Broad Wy

PO

Highfield Ter

Broad Wy

River Parrett Trail

BOWER HINTON B3165

North

Kings Rd

Bind Lane

Middle St

Hotel

3 46

47

Back Lane

A   B   C   D

Higher St

B3161

30

Ringwell Hill

er Parrett Tr

A303

Works

West Stoke

Glovers Cl

Ash

Back Street

Burrough Street

E

Middle Leaze Drove

F

48

G

49

H urnfield

Quarry

A303

I

Little Trumps

20

2

Tintinhu

Hallets Orchar

Head

Incombe Wy

PO

Montacute Road

Foldhill Lane

A303

Halfway House Farm

Marsh Lane

3

urlocks

22

19

Perren's Hill Farm

4

Trutts Brook

A3088

Wellham's Mill

Marsh Lane

Wellhams Brook

5

118

Stoke Sub
Har don

48

E

F

31

East
Stoke

Mulberry Lane

Marsh Lane

G

49

H

A3088

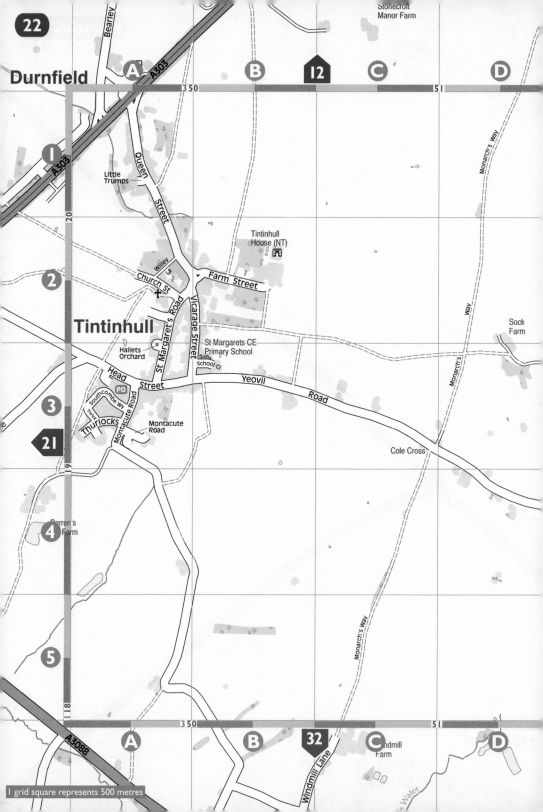

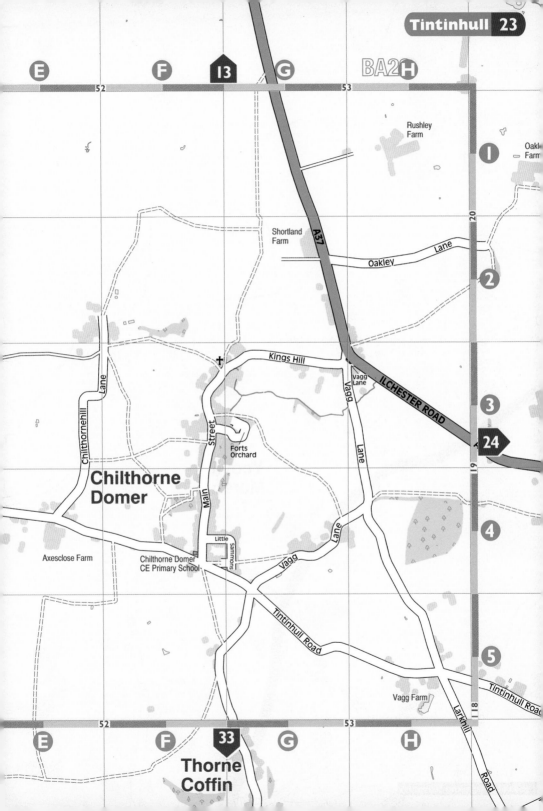

E F **13** G BA2 H

52 53

Rushley
Farm

Oakl
Farm

I

20

Shortland
Farm

A37

Oakley Lane

2

Kings Hill

Vagg
Lane

ILCHESTER ROAD

Vagg Lane

3

Chilthornehill Lane

Street

Forts
Orchard

24

19

**Chilthorne
Domer**

Lane

Vagg

4

Axesclose Farm

Little
Sammons

Chilthorne Domer
CE Primary School

Vagg

Lane

Tintinhull Road

5

Vagg Farm

Larkhill Road

Tintinhull Road

118

52 53

E F **33** G H

**Thorne
Coffin**

24

A   B   **14**   C   D

3 54   55

Rushley
Farm

I

Oakley
Farms

20

Lane

2

3

3

ESTER ROAD

23

A37

19

Woodrows
Farm

Greenmoor Lane

4

Yeovil
Marsh
†

Poplars Cl

Orchard Cl

Chapel La

Chapel La

5

Marsh Lane

Larkhill Rd

18

Tintinhull Road

Coppits Hill

ILCHESTER ROAD

A37

Lane

Marshes
Hill Farm

g Farm

A   B   **34**   C   D

3 54   55

BA21

Thorne Lane

Thorne La

1 grid square represents 500 metres

Ⓐ 358 Ⓑ **16** Ⓒ 59 Ⓓ

Hinton

Somerset County
Dorset County

A359

Ⓘ

20

PO

Ⓩ

Hale's Meadow

Hummer
Farm

Thorny Lane

Birch

A359

Monarch's Way

Ⓒ

Gore

Ⓒ

Cemetery

25

19

Monarch's Way

Manor
Farm

River Yeo

Primrose
La

Ⓐ

Up Mudford

Primrose Lane

Monarch's Way

Youngs
Endowed
Primary School

Fisher's Cl

Church
Farm

PH

Ⓒ

Dorset County
Somerset County

Ⓣ

18

Trent Brooks

Mill
Lane

Ⓐ 358 Ⓑ **36** Ⓒ 59 Ⓓ

Trent Cl

edwood Road

Wit

sandicr

E   F   **17**   G   H

Pitfield   Corner

White Post

Great Pit Lane

Lane

Great Pit Lane

Road

Middle   Lane

I

Moorw

60   61

B3148

ON HILL

dber

Rowbarrow   Hill

Rowbarrow Hill

Penmore

Penmore   Road

20

2

Birch Hill

B3148

3

28

19

Ham Lane

Patson Hill Lane

4

Rigg   Lane

Malthouse Lane

Ham   Lane

Ham Lane

Trent Barrow

nt

Lane

Plot Lane

Down Lane

Monarch's   Way

Monarch's Way

18

Co

5

60   61

E   F   **37**   G   H

E   64   F   **19**   G   65   H

B3145

Poyntington **1**

The Ridge

20

Red
Post

2

mbe

Clatcombe Lane

B3145

3

Lower Boyston Lane

4

Rechole Lane

B3145

Oborne

5

118

E   64   F   **39**   G   65   H

The Gryphon
School

St Aldhelm's Road

ROAD B3145

Castle Town Way

Coldharbour
Business Park

Blackmarsh
Farm

A30

30

Broad Way
Broad Wy
ston's
ne

Blind Lane

A Hotel

Highfield Ter
PO

†

River Parrett Trail

B

20

River Parrett Trail

C

North
Combe Rd

D

3 46

47

BOWER HINTON

Middle St

Works

Lack Lane

Higher St

B3165

RINGWELL HILL

West Stoke

Glovers Cl

Cole La

Great Field Lane

Cole La

Tiptoft
Beck's Fd
W's Cl

Works

I

Cripple
Hill

Ringwell Hill

A303

Works

†

Stoke
Priory

The Avenue

Langlands

VW
Cl

Hill

2

Small Moor Brook

A303

West Street

Works

Hamdon
La

Hamdon
Medical Ce

Matt's La

etherton
ridge

3

PROPHET'S LANE

West Street

Norton Road

TA14

River Parrett

4

A356

New Road

**Norton
Sub Ham**

Norton Sub- Hamdon
CE Primary School

Hamdon VW

Orch Barn

Great Street

Works †

Glebelands

5

Higher Street

Little Street

Church La

Rectory La

Skinner's Lane

Broadmead

PO

Minchington's
Close

Little
Mead

Barrows
Lane

River Parrett Trail

A

3 46

River Parrett Trail

B

A356

C

47

D

Manor Farm

I grid square represents 500 metres

E

F

21

G

H

48

49

18

A3088

Stoke Sub Hamdon

East Stoke

I

n

Street

's

Street

Mulberry Lane

Windsor

East Stonehill Stoke

Lane

Marsh Lane

Wellh Brook

ok

Stanchester Community School

Montacute

Mason Lane

Hyde Rd

Lwr Hyde Rd

Hyde Road

Road

2

Bishopston

Wash

PH

Midd St

17

Trail

✝

Trail

Monarch's Way

Hedgecock Hill

Monarch's Way

St Michael's Hill

Monarch's Way

Montacute

3

T

Park VW

Townsen

Leland

Trail

Road

Ham Hill Country Park

32

Lan

Hollow

4

Park La

Liberty Trail

Liberty Trail

Liberty Trail

16

5

Little Norton

Liberty

48

Liberty Trail

Trail

Westbury Farm

49

E

F

G

H

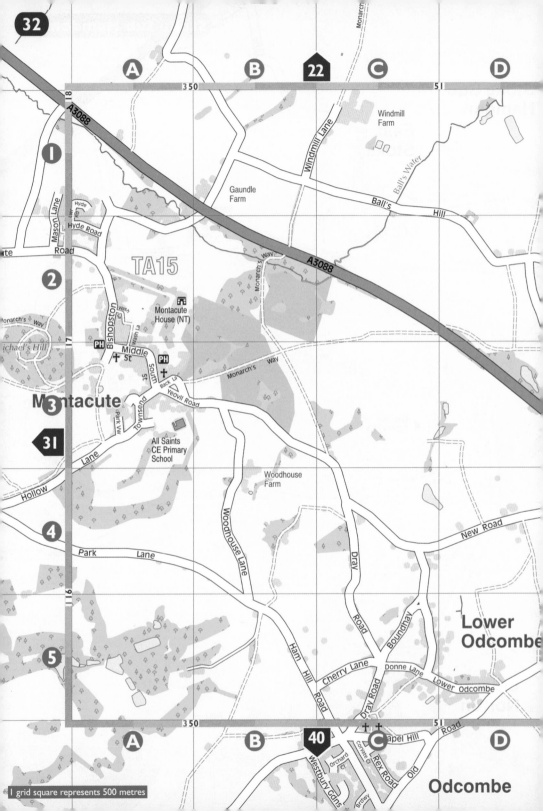

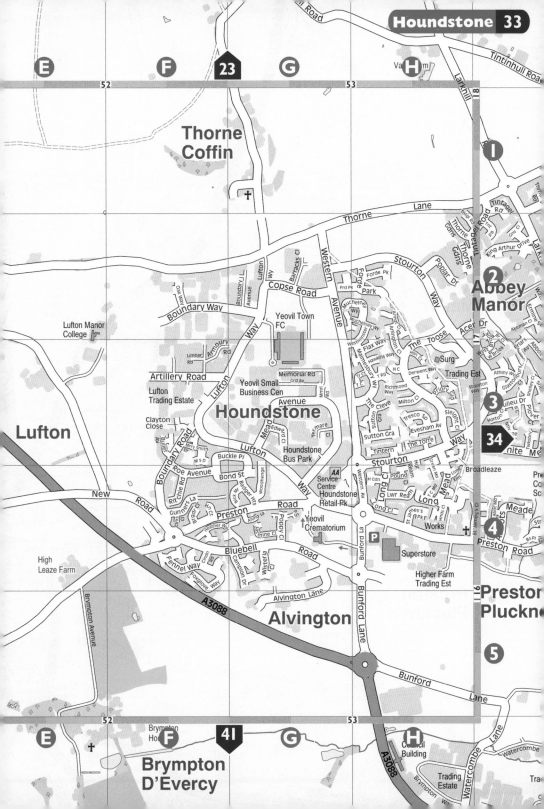

E   52   F   23   G   53   H   Tintinhull Road

Thorne
Coffin

I

Thorne   Lane   Tintagel Rd

Western   Stourton   2
Copse Road   Avenue   Abbey Manor

Boundary Way   The Toose

Lufton Manor
College   Yeovil Town
FC   Surg   Trading Est

Artillery Road   Memorial Rd
Lufton   Yeovil Small   Grd Av   3
Trading Estate   Business Cen
                                      Richmond Way

Lufton   **Houndstone**   Avenue   Milton Cl   34

Clayton   Tresco Sq
Close   Evesham Av
                      Lufton   Sutton Gra
                                      Tintern   The Torre
                      Buckle Pl
          Roe Avenue Bond St   Stourton   Broadleaze
New   Road   Long
          Ritchie Rd   AA
          Preston   Service   Way
                                      Centre
                                      Houndstone
                      Bluebell   Retail Pk
High   Yeovil   4
Leaze Farm Fennel Way   Crematorium   Preston Road
                                      P
                      Road   Superstore   Preston
                                                          Pluckne
          A3088   Alvington Lane
                                      Higher Farm   5
                      Alvington   Trading Est

                      Bunford   Bunford
                                               Lane

E   52   F   41   G   53   H   Council
                                      Building
✝   A3088   Trading   Watercombe
Brymton Brympton   Estate
D'Evercy Ho

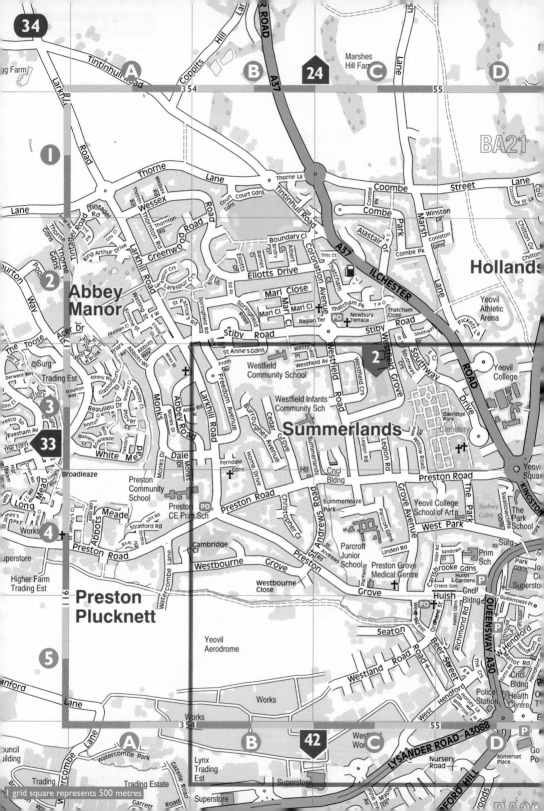

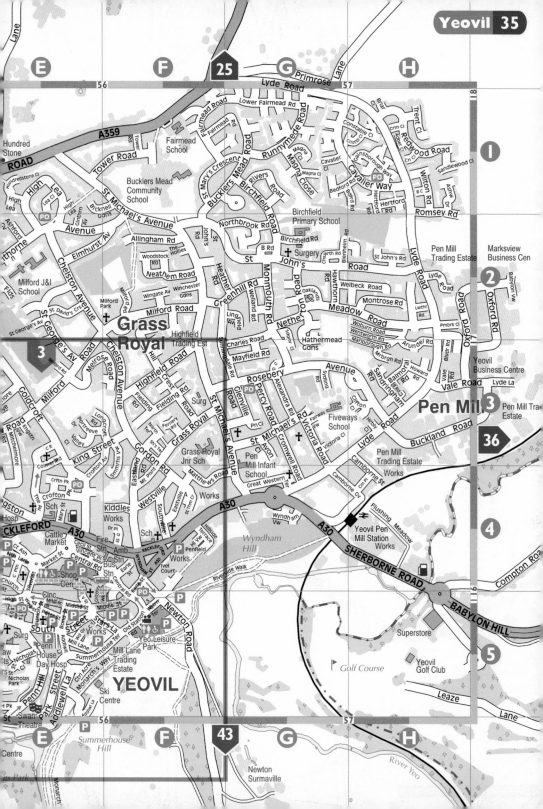

A 358 B 26 C 59 D

Trent Brook

Mill La

Ne
Co

Trent Cl
Redwood Rd
Cn Cl
1
Sandlewood Cl
Wilton Rd
B Cl
Ashw Dr
Romsey Rd

Net
Cor

Lyde Road

Pen Mill
Trading Estate
Marksview
Business Cen

Babylon Vw

Over
Compt

Lyde
2
Road
117ford Road
Oxford Rd
Western Street

Lwthr
Rd
Pmbrk Cl

Yeovil
Business Centre
Lyde La

St
Michaels

Over
Compt

Arundel Rd
Blvar Rd
Howard
Rd
Vale Road

Compton Road

Butte
House

Pen Mill
3
Pen Mill Trading
Estate

Marl

Buck
35
Estate

Lane

4

Compton Road

A30

ROAD
BABYLON HILL

uperstore

5
Yeovil
Golf Club

Leaze
Lane

East
Farm

A 358 B 44 C 59 D

Underdown Hollow

er Yeo

1 grid square represents 500 metres

E   F   **27**   G   H

60   61

Monarch's Way

18

I

Tucker's
Cross

2

17

Crossfields
Elly
La

Crssfld

Plum Orch

(Track)

Hart's La

Ratleigh Lane

Gooseland Lane

Stallen

3

38

Compton Road

Lane

Ratleigh / Lane

4

BABYLON HILL   A30

Low's

16

Halfway
House

Hill Lane

Noor Farm

5

Bedmill Farm

Silverlake
Farm

E   F   **45**   G   H

60   61

E F 29 G H

64 65 18

The Gryphon School

St Aldhelm's Road

Coldharbour Business Park

Castle Town Way

Blackmarsh Farm

Quarr Dr Strand

McCreery Rd

St Pauls Green

St Pauls Ct

Granville Way

Coldharbour Hosp

COLD HARBOUR A30

I

Vernalls Road

Sherborne Prim Sch

Simons Rd

Granville Way

Business Park

OBORNE ROAD B3145

Kings Road

Harbour Way

Wooton Ct

Harbour Rd

Lambsfield

Landgons

Works

PO

Kings Cts

A30

Hill

Earls Cl

Chandlers

Castle Road

Castle Town Way

2

Grove Medical Cen

COLD HARBOUR

NORTH ROAD

The Avenue

DT9

House

Tinneys Lane

Pinford L

GREENHILL

Cr Sta

Newland

St SWITHIN'S

Tinneys Lane

Knotts Paddck

Castleton Road

Pinford Lane

Sherborne Old Castle

3

Hospital Lane

Newld

St Swithins

The Wilderness

B3145

CHEAP STREET

PO

Hound Street

Abbey Rd

School

B3145

LONG STREET

Medical Centre

East Mill Lane

Hotel

Sherborne Lake

Sherborne Museum

M

Sherborne Abbey

Works

Sherborne Castle

PH

Hlf Mn St

Police Stn

Ludbourne Rd

Superstore

New Road

4

Trendle

PH

Digby Road

SOUTH STREET

Pageant Dr

LC

Works

Acreman

Durrant Cl

Station Rd

Sherborne Station

Home Farm

Riverside Works

Acreman Street

NEW ROAD

B3145

Sherborne FC

Dancing Hill

The Kennels

Gainsborough Hill

5

A352

64 65

E F 47 G H

SHERBO

16

E F **33** G H

52 53

Bunford Lane

Brympton House

Brympton D'Evercy

Council Building

Trading Estate

Trad

I

Sea King Road Ga

A3088 LYSA

Broadleaze Farm

A3088

Ashmead

Watercombe Lane

A308 WATERCOMBE LANE

Laburnum Way

Oakleigh

Birchdale Ridgemea

The Spinney

2

Coppice Cl

St Mtns Wy

Watercombe Hts

Rye Gdns

Nathar

Camp Hill

Camp Road

Feebarrow

WEST COKER ROAD

Hotel

Wyvern Close

Helena Rd

Priory Cl

Pl.
La

Nash

3

42

Gooseacre Lane

A30

Green Lane

West Coker

Manor Farm

Lane

Surg

4

HIGH STREET

Cedar Flds

Denzil Cl

Church St

Manor St

Works

Burto

Brdcrs

Broadacres Cres

Burton La

Long

Furlong

Meadow Vw

Burt

PO

Orchard Close

East

Street

Manor Dr

Laurel Cl

Ryefields Cl

Mill Lane

Mill Lane

5

PO

Mill Close

Ruddock Wy

Cheshels Cl

Ruddock Wy

Font Villas

Lakefields

Halves Lane

Holywell

Hal 53s

Mill Lane

Drks Mdw

E F G H

52 53

Halves Lane

Mill

Ridg

Primrose Hill

Lane

ardington

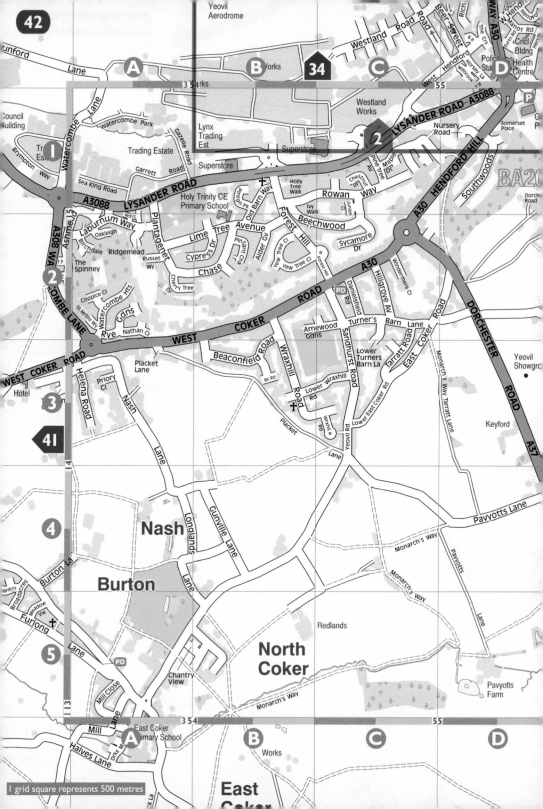

I grid square represents 500 metres

YEOVIL

Newton Surmaville

Two Tower Lane

Newton Road

Golf Course

Yeovil Golf Club

Leaze Lane

River Yeo

Superstore

Jack the Treacle Eater

Barwick House

Rex's Lane

Yeo Valley

Yeovil Junction Station

Clifton Maubank

Barbarians UFC

Cemetery

Hotel

Hillside View

Barwick

Barwick County Primary School

Court Lane

Meadow View

Acres Ct

Newton Road

Clifton Hill

Bridle Way

PO

Whitcross

Court Lane

New Road

Stoford

Road

Higher Bullen

Clifton Vw

Silver Street

Hooper's Lane

Fairhouse Lane

Cowpool Farm

Entertainment Complex

Mill Lane Trading Estate

Summerhouse Way

Monarch's Way

Ski Centre

Penn House

Day Hosp

Nicholas Park

Swan Theatre

Summerhouse Hill

Addlewell La

Park Street

Monarch's Way

35

44

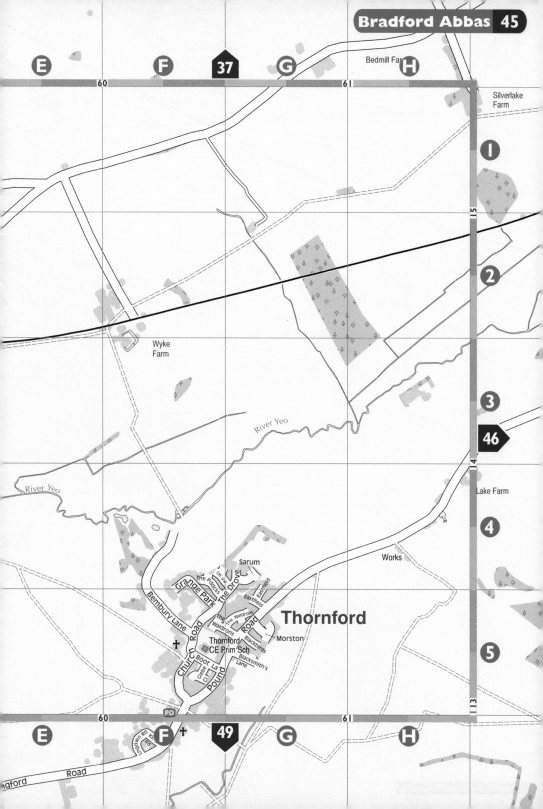

E   F   **37**   G   Bedmill Farm   H

Silverlake Farm

I

15

2

Wyke Farm

3

River Yeo

46

14

Lake Farm

4

River Yeo

Works

Sarum

Grange Park

The Paddocks

Oak View

The Drove

Eastfield

Eastfield

Thornford

Bembury Lane

Church Road

The Firs

Waldrons

Waldrons

Road

Blackbirds

Morston

5

Thornford
CE Prim Sch

Blacksmith's Lane

Boot La

Glebe Cl

Pound La

113

†

PO

E   F   **49**   G   H

Longford Rd

Kiln Lane

gford   Road

46

A 3 62 **B** **38** **C** 63 **D**

Lenthay
Dairy House

Honeycombe

Silverlake
Farm

Sherborne Abbey
CE Primary School

Works

West

Mill

1

*Lenthay
Common*

LC

15

Honeycombe
Farm

2

*Honeycombe
Wood*

Court
House Dairy

3

45

14

Lake Farm

4

5

13

Higher
Farm

Gordon's

Lane

Lillington

Higher Street

A 3 62 **B** 63 **C** **D**

Lower Street

B3145 NEW

A35

Sherborne
FC

Dancing Hill

The Kennels

E

F

39

G

H

64

65

SHERBORNE HILL

Gainsborough Hill

I

Macmillan Way

A352

A3030

15

West Lane

2

Nor
Wo

Westhill
Lodge

Macmillan Way

3

A30

14

Leweston
Farm

4

Folke La

Newcross

Newcross

Kings
Cl

Kings
Close

Kings
Lane

Quarry
Lane

Longburton

Broke Lane

5

13

E

F

G

Spring
La

H

West
Hall

64

65

A352

†

A 3 58 **B** 44 **C** 59 **D**

13

1

Clifton Farm

Clifton Wood

2

12

Trill Lane

Thornford Station

Trill Farm

3

4

Thornford Road

St Andrews CE Primary School

Coles La

Stonyacres

Clvrmd

Clovermead

Bucklers Mead

5

Down's Lane

Church Farm

†

Ryme Intrinseca

Ryme Road

Uplands

High St

Queen St

High St

Melbury Road

St Ormund's Cl

Birch Lane

Tark's Hill

Common Lane

Bakegate Lane

A 3 58 **B** 59 **C** **D**

1 grid square represents 500 metres

Beer Hackett

Knighton

Whitfield Farm

Whitfield Woods

Thornford CE Prim Sch

Morston

Blackbirds

Blacksmith's Lane

Boot La

Church Road

Pound

King's Rd

London Rd

oford Road

Claypits Lane

Macmillan Way

Yetminster Station

Works

Sussex Farm Wy

Brierley Hay

Eastlands

Willow Farm

Macmillan Way

Church Cl

nster

Brister End

Downs La

Shearstones

E F G H

45

PO

60 61

I3

I2

I1

I 2 3 4 5

60 61

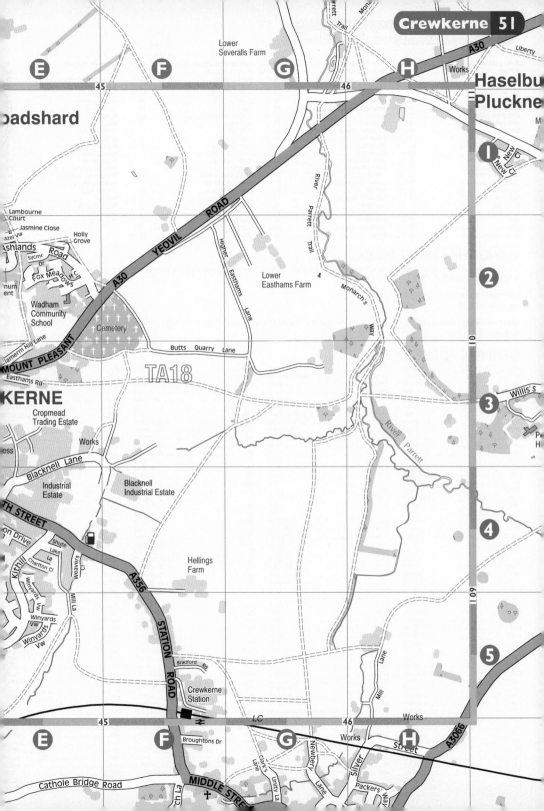

E F G H

Lower
Severalls Farm

A30

Works

Haselbu
Pluckne

New
Ci
New Ci

I

M

badshard

YEOVIL ROAD

River Parrett Trail

Lambourne
Court
Jasmine Close
azel Vw
Holly
Grove
ashlands
Road
sycmr
Dr
Fox Meadows
num
ent

A30

Wadham
Community
School

Cemetery

Lower
Easthams Farm

Higher Easthams Lane

Monarch's Way

2

amerm Hill Lane

MOUNT PLEASANT

Butts Quarry Lane

Easthams Rd

TA18

Willis's

KERNE

Cropmead
Trading Estate

Works

River Parrett

3

P
H

Blacknell Lane

Industrial
Estate

Blacknell
Industrial Estate

ess

4

TH STREET

on Drive

shute
Lake
La

Kithill

Charlton Cl

Weavers

A356

Hellings
Farm

Mill La

Winyards Vw

Winyards
Vw

Winyards
Vw

STATION ROAD

Bradford Rd

5

Lane

Mill

Crewkerne
Station

LC

Works

E F G H

Broughtons Dr

Newbery Lane

Works

Silver Street

A3066

Cathole Bridge Road

MIDDLE STRE

Clark's Lane

Unity La

Packers Way

45 46 10 60 09

Abbey Manor	34 A2	Heaven's Door	17 H4
Adber	27 E1	Higher Sandford	28 B1
Alvington	33 G5	Hinton	25 H1
Ashington	15 F4	Hollands	34 D2
Barwick	43 F4	Holway	28 D1
Beer Hackett	49 E2	Holywell	41 G5
Bower Hinton	20 A5	Houndstone	33 G3
Bradford Abbas	44 B3	Hurst	20 A4
Bridgehampton	8 B3	Ilchester	13 F1
Broadshard	50 D1	Ilchester Mead	13 E2
Brookhampton	5 H1	Knighton	49 H4
Brympton D'Evercy	41 F1	Lillington	46 C5
Burton	42 A4	Limington	14 B2
Chilthorne Domer	23 E4	Little Norton	31 E5
Chilton Cantelo	15 H3	Little Weston	5 F5
Clifton Maybank	44 A4	Longburton	47 G5
Corton Denham	19 E2	Lower Odcombe	32 D5
Crewkerne	50 D3	Lufton	33 E3
Downhead	8 C1	Marston Magna	16 C1
Draycott	14 C3	Martock	20 A2
East Stoke	31 F1	Montacute	31 H3
Girt	11 G4	Mudford	25 H2
Gore	26 D3	Mudford Sock	25 E3
Grass Royal	3 K2	Nash	42 A4
Nether Compton	36 D1	Stockwitch Cross	8
North Cadbury	5 H2	Stoford	43
North Coker	42 B5	Stoke Sub Hamdon	31
Northover	6 A5	Summerlands	2
Norton Sub Hamdon	30 D4	Sutton Montis	11
Oborne	29 H5	Thorne Coffin	33
Odcombe	40 C1	Thornford	45
Over Compton	36 D2	Tintinhull	22
Parkway	17 E3	Trent	26
Pen Mill	35 H3	Up Mudford	26
Podimore	7 F2	Urgashay	8
Poyntington	29 H1	Wales	9
Preston Plucknett	34 A5	West Camel	9
Queen Camel	9 H2	West Coker	41
Rimpton	17 H3	West Mudford	25
Ryme Intrinseca	48 B5	Weston Bampfylde	10
Sandford Orcas	18 B5	West Stoke	30
Sherborne	38 C3	Whitcombe	11
South Barrow	4 B1	Yeovil	3
South Cadbury	5 G5	Yeovil Marsh	24
Sparkford	4 C4	Yeovilton	14
Speckington	8 B4	Yetminster	48
Stafford's Green	18 D4		
Stallen	37 G3		

USING THE STREET INDEX

Street names are listed alphabetically. Each street name is followed by its postal town or area locality, the Postcode District, the page number, and the reference to the square in which the name is found.

Standard index entries are shown as follows:

Abbey Rd *SHER* DT9 ....**39** E3

Street names and selected addresses not shown on the map due to scale restrictions are shown in the index with an asterisk:

Bartlett Pl *YEON* * BA21 ....**34** A4

GENERAL ABBREVIATIONS

ACC	ACCESS	E	EAST	LDG	LODGE	R	RIVE
ALY	ALLEY	EMB	EMBANKMENT	LGT	LIGHT	RBT	ROUNDABOU
AP	APPROACH	EMBY	EMBASSY	LK	LOCK	RD	ROA
AR	ARCADE	ESP	ESPLANADE	LKS	LAKES	RDG	RIDG
ASS	ASSOCIATION	EST	ESTATE	LNDG	LANDING	REP	REPUBLI
AV	AVENUE	EX	EXCHANGE	LTL	LITTLE	RES	RESERVOI
BCH	BEACH	EXPY	EXPRESSWAY	LWR	LOWER	RFC	RUGBY FOOTBALL CLU
BLDS	BUILDINGS	EXT	EXTENSION	MAG	MAGISTRATE	RI	RIS
BND	BEND	F/O	FLYOVER	MAN	MANSIONS	RP	RAM
BNK	BANK	FC	FOOTBALL CLUB	MD	MEAD	RW	RO
BR	BRIDGE	FK	FORK	MDW	MEADOWS	S	SOUT
BRK	BROOK	FLD	FIELD	MEM	MEMORIAL	SCH	SCHOO
BTM	BOTTOM	FLDS	FIELDS	MKT	MARKET	SE	SOUTH EAS
BUS	BUSINESS	FLS	FALLS	MKTS	MARKETS	SER	SERVICE ARE
BVD	BOULEVARD	FLS	FLATS	ML	MALL	SH	SHOR
BY	BYPASS	FM	FARM	ML	MILL	SHOP	SHOPPIN
CATH	CATHEDRAL	FT	FORT	MNR	MANOR	SKWY	SKYWA
CEM	CEMETERY	FWY	FREEWAY	MS	MEWS	SMT	SUMMI
CEN	CENTRE	FY	FERRY	MSN	MISSION	SOC	SOCIET
CFT	CROFT	GA	GATE	MT	MOUNT	SP	SPU
CH	CHURCH	GAL	GALLERY	MTN	MOUNTAIN	SPR	SPRIN
CHA	CHASE	GDN	GARDEN	MTS	MOUNTAINS	SQ	SQUAR
CHYD	CHURCHYARD	GDNS	GARDENS	MUS	MUSEUM	ST	STREE
CIR	CIRCLE	GLD	GLADE	MWY	MOTORWAY	STN	STATIO
CIRC	CIRCUS	GLN	GLEN	N	NORTH	STR	STREA
CL	CLOSE	GN	GREEN	NE	NORTH EAST	STRD	STRAN
CLFS	CLIFFS	GND	GROUND	NW	NORTH WEST	SW	SOUTH WE
CMP	CAMP	GRA	GRANGE	O/P	OVERPASS	TDG	TRADIN
CNR	CORNER	GRG	GARAGE	OFF	OFFICE	TER	TERRAC
CO	COUNTY	GT	GREAT	ORCH	ORCHARD	THWY	THROUGHWA
COLL	COLLEGE	GTWY	GATEWAY	OV	OVAL	TNL	TUNNE
COM	COMMON	GV	GROVE	PAL	PALACE	TOLL	TOLLWA
COMM	COMMISSION	HGR	HIGHER	PAS	PASSAGE	TPK	TURNPIK
CON	CONVENT	HL	HILL	PAV	PAVILION	TR	TRAC
COT	COTTAGE	HLS	HILLS	PDE	PARADE	TRL	TRAI
COTS	COTTAGES	HO	HOUSE	PH	PUBLIC HOUSE	TWR	TOWE
CP	CAPE	HOL	HOLLOW	PK	PARK	U/P	UNDERPAS
CPS	COPSE	HOSP	HOSPITAL	PKWY	PARKWAY	UNI	UNIVERSIT
CR	CREEK	HRB	HARBOUR	PL	PLACE	UPR	UPPE
CREM	CREMATORIUM	HTH	HEATH	PLN	PLAIN	V	VAL
CRS	CRESCENT	HTS	HEIGHTS	PLNS	PLAINS	VA	VALLE
CSWY	CAUSEWAY	HVN	HAVEN	PLZ	PLAZA	VIAD	VIADUC
CT	COURT	HWY	HIGHWAY	POL	POLICE STATION	VIL	VILL
CTRL	CENTRAL	IMP	IMPERIAL	PR	PRINCE	VIS	VIST
CTS	COURTS	IN	INLET	PREC	PRECINCT	VLG	VILLAG
CTYD	COURTYARD	IND EST	INDUSTRIAL ESTATE	PREP	PREPARATORY	VLS	VILLAS
CUTT	CUTTINGS	INF	INFIRMARY	PRIM	PRIMARY	VW	VIEW
CV	COVE	INFO	INFORMATION	PROM	PROMENADE	W	WES
CYN	CANYON	INT	INTERCHANGE	PRS	PRINCESS	WD	WOO
DEPT	DEPARTMENT	IS	ISLAND	PRT	PORT	WHF	WHAR
DL	DALE	JCT	JUNCTION	PT	POINT	WK	WAL
DM	DAM	JTY	JETTY	PTH	PATH	WKS	WALK
DR	DRIVE	KG	KING	PZ	PIAZZA	WLS	WELL
DRO	DROVE	KNL	KNOLL	QD	QUADRANT	WY	WA
DRY	DRIVEWAY	L	LAKE	QU	QUEEN	YD	YAR
DWGS	DWELLINGS	LA	LANE	QY	QUAY	YHA	YOUTH HOSTE

OSTCODE TOWNS AND AREA ABBREVIATIONS

EWK ....Crewkerne
UTE ....Montacute
TK ....Martock

RYEO ....Rural Yeovil
SHER ....Sherborne
SOM ....Somerton

SPETH ....South Petherton
SSH ....Stoke Sub Hamdon
YEON ....Yeovil north

YEOS ....Yeovil south

Index - streets

Abb - Cyp

A

bey Rd SHER DT9 ....39 E3
YEON BA21 ....34 A3
bey St CREWK TA18 ....50 C3
bots Meade YEON BA21 ....34 A4
bots Wy SHER DT9 ....38 C4
YEON BA21 ....34 A3
botts Rd RYEO BA22 ....13 E1
els La SHER DT9 ....27 E4
er Dr YEON BA21 ....33 H2
reman Ct SHER DT9 ....38 D3
reman Pl SHER DT9 ....39 E4
reman St SHER DT9 ....38 D3
e Acres MRTK TA12 ....20 B2
res Ct RYEO BA22 ....43 G4
ber Cl YEON BA21 ....35 H1
dlewell La YEOS DT9 ....3 H6
mirals Cl SHER DT9 ....39 F2
eman La YEON BA21 ....34 A4
astair Cl YEON BA21 ....34 C2
astair Dr YEON BA21 ....34 C2
pany Cl SHER DT9 ....39 F1
bert Cl YEON BA21 ....34 B2
der Gv CREWK TA18 ....50 D1
YEOS BA20 ....42 B2
dondale Gdns YEOS BA20 ....3 G7
exandra Rd YEON BA21 ....35 G3
ingham Rd YEON BA21 ....35 F2
otment Rd RYEO BA22 ....11 G2
nshouse La RYEO BA22 ....13 F1
vington La RYEO BA22 ....33 G5
mbrose Cl SHER DT9 ....44 C2
lington Cl YEON BA21 ....33 H2
moury Rd RYEO BA22 ....33 F3
newood Gdns YEOS BA20 ....42 B2
tillery Rd RYEO BA22 ....33 F3
undel Rd YEON BA21 ....35 H3
hfield Pk MRTK TA12 ....20 B3
hford Gv YEON BA21 ....35 E2
hington La RYEO BA22 ....25 E3
hland Ct CREWK TA18 ....50 D2
hlands Cl CREWK TA18 ....50 D2
hlands Meadow
CREWK TA18 ....50 D1
hlands Rd CREWK TA18 ....51 E2
hmead YEOS BA20 ....41 H2
hwood Dr YEON BA21 ....35 H1
kwith Cl SHER DT9 ....38 C5
pen Wy CREWK TA18 ....50 D2
helney Wy YEON BA21 ....34 A3
antic Wy RYEO BA22 ....7 G4
e Avenue RYEO BA22 ....4 C4
SHER DT9 ....39 F2
SSH TA14 ....30 D2
YEON BA21 ....3 G3
on Cl YEON BA21 ....35 G3

B

bylon Hl YEON BA21 ....35 H5
bylon Vw YEON BA21 ....36 A2
ck La MCUTE TA15 ....32 A3
RYEO BA22 ....13 F1
RYEO BA22 ....17 G3
RYEO BA22 ....40 A5
SHER DT9 ....39 E3
SHER DT9 ....44 C3
ck St RYEO BA22 ....9 E2
dger Hts RYEO BA22 ....33 G4
akehouse La SHER DT9 ....44 C3
all's Hl MCUTE TA15 ....32 C1
almoral Rd YEON BA21 ....35 H3
rlynch Ct YEON BA21 ....34 A3
arn Cl CREWK TA18 ....50 C4
rnet Cl YEON BA21 ....34 B2
rn St CREWK TA18 ....50 C4
rracks Cl RYEO BA22 ....33 G2
rrows La SSH TA14 ....30 C5
rtlett Pl YEON * BA21 ....34 A4
rtletts Pl YEON BA21 ....34 A4
rton Gdns SHER DT9 ....38 C3
aconfield Rd YEOS BA20 ....42 B3

Beacon La SHER DT9 ....11 H4
Bearley Bridge Rd MRTK TA12 ....20 B2
Bearley La RYEO BA22 ....12 A5
Bearley Rd MRTK TA12 ....20 C3
Beaulieu Dr YEON BA21 ....34 A3
Becks Fld SSH TA14 ....30 D1
Bedford Rd YEON BA21 ....35 G1
The Beeches YEON * BA21 ....2 E1
Beech Rd MRTK TA12 ....20 B2
Beechwood YEOS BA20 ....42 B2
Beechwood Dr CREWK TA18 ....50 D2
Beer St YEOS BA20 ....6 E1
Belvedere Rd YEON BA21 ....35 H3
Bembury La SHER DT9 ....45 F5
Berkeley Rd YEOS BA20 ....2 E6
Bicknell Gdns YEON BA21 ....35 E1
Bincombe Dr CREWK TA18 ....50 D1
Bindwell La RYEO BA22 ....10 A3
Bineham La RYEO BA22 ....6 D5
Birchdale YEOS BA20 ....42 A2
Birchfield Rd YEON BA21 ....35 G1
Birch La SHER DT9 ....48 D5
Birch Rd MRTK TA12 ....20 B2
Bird's Cl CREWK TA18 ....50 C3
Bishop's La SHER DT9 ....44 C2
Bishopston MCUTE TA15 ....32 A3
Bishops Wk RYEO BA22 ....13 E1
Blackberry La SHER DT9 ....39 E2
Blackbirds SHER DT9 ....9 E1
Black Mere RYEO BA22 ....33 G4
Blacknell La CREWK TA18 ....51 E4
Blacksmith's La SHER DT9 ....45 G5
Blackthorne Cl RYEO BA22 ....6 B4
Blackwell Rd RYEO BA22 ....9 G2
Blake Rd CREWK TA18 ....50 D4
Blenheim Rd YEON BA21 ....35 G2
Blind La MRTK TA12 ....20 A5
Bluebell Rd RYEO BA22 ....33 F4
Bond St RYEO BA22 ....33 H4
YEON BA20 ....3 H5
Bonnie's La SSH TA14 ....31 E1
Boot La SHER DT9 ....45 F5
Boreland La RYEO BA22 ....14 B3
The Borough Ar YEOS * BA20 ....3 C5
Boundary Av RYEO BA22 ....33 G2
Boundary Rd RYEO BA22 ....33 F4
Boundary Wy RYEO BA22 ....33 F2
Boundhay RYEO BA22 ....33 C5
Bowditch Rw CREWK * TA18 ....50 D3
Bower Ct SHER DT9 ....49 E5
Bower Hinton MRTK TA12 ....30 A1
Bowhayes CREWK TA18 ....50 D4
Bowleaze YEON BA21 ....34 A3
Bracey Rd MRTK TA12 ....20 B1
Bradford Rd CREWK TA18 ....51 F5
SHER DT9 ....38 B4
Brains La RYEO BA22 ....4 C4
Bramley Cl CREWK TA18 ....50 D1
Briar Cl YEON BA21 ....35 H1
Briarfield RYEO BA22 ....6 B4
Brick Yard La CREWK TA18 ....50 D2
Bridge Ri MRTK TA12 ....20 C2
Bridle Wy RYEO BA22 ....43 F5
Brierley Hay SHER DT9 ....49 E5
Brigadier Cl RYEO BA22 ....33 F4
Bristol Rd SHER DT9 ....39 E1
Broadacres RYEO BA22 ....41 H5
Broadlands Cl YEON BA21 ....35 H1
Broadleaze YEON BA21 ....33 H4
Broadmead La SSH TA14 ....30 D5
Broadshard Rd CREWK TA18 ....50 D1
Broadway RYEO BA22 ....40 C1
Brook Cl YEON BA21 ....34 A2
Brookside RYEO BA22 ....41 E4
Brunswick St YEOS BA20 ....3 F6
Brympton Av RYEO BA22 ....33 E5
Brympton Wy YEOS BA20 ....41 H1
Buckhill Cl CREWK TA18 ....50 D5
Buckland La RYEO BA22 ....11 G2
Buckland Rd YEON BA21 ....35 H3
Buckle Pl RYEO BA22 ....33 F3
Bucklers Md SHER DT9 ....48 C5
Bucklers Mead Rd YEON BA21 ....35 F1
Buller Av RYEO BA22 ....33 F3

Bulls La CREWK TA18 ....50 C3
Bunford La YEOS BA20 ....33 H4
Burlingham's La RYEO BA22 ....12 C3
Burroughes Av YEON BA21 ....2 A2
Burton La RYEO BA22 ....41 H4
Bushfield Rd CREWK TA18 ....50 C5
Butts Quarry La CREWK TA18 ....51 F3

C

Camborne Gv YEON BA21 ....35 G4
Camborne Pl YEON BA21 ....35 H4
Camborne St YEON BA21 ....35 H3
Camel St RYEO BA22 ....9 H5
Campion Dr RYEO BA22 ....33 G4
Camp Rd RYEO BA22 ....40 C2
Canons Ga RYEO BA22 ....13 E1
Carisbrooke Gdns YEOS BA20 ....2 D4
Carpenters Ter MRTK * TA12 ....20 A5
Carters La RYEO BA22 ....40 A5
Cary Rd RYEO BA22 ....9 H2
Castle La RYEO BA22 ....11 H1
Castle Rd SHER DT9 ....39 G2
Castle St SSH TA14 ....30 D1
Castleton Rd SHER DT9 ....39 F3
Castle Town Wy SHER DT9 ....29 E5
Cathole Bridge Rd
CREWK TA18 ....50 A4
Cavalier Cl YEON BA21 ....35 G1
Cavalier Wy YEON BA21 ....35 G1
Cecil St YEOS BA20 ....3 H4
Cedar Ct MRTK TA12 ....20 B1
Cedar Flds RYEO BA22 ....41 E4
Cedar Gv YEON BA21 ....2 B2
Celandine Rd RYEO BA22 ....33 F4
Central Acre YEOS BA20 ....3 H6
Central Av YEOS BA20 ....6 A4
Central Rd YEOS BA20 ....3 H4
Chandlers SHER DT9 ....39 F2
Channel Dash Pl RYEO BA22 ....6 A4
Chantry La RYEO BA22 ....8 D3
Chantry Vw RYEO BA22 ....42 A5
Chapel Hl RYEO BA22 ....40 C1
Chapel La RYEO BA22 ....4 A1
RYEO BA22 ....5 H1
SHER DT9 ....49 E5
YEON BA21 ....24 B5
Chapel Meadow SHER DT9 ....48 D5
Chard Rd CREWK TA18 ....50 A3
Charles Rd YEON BA21 ....35 G4
Charlton Cl CREWK TA18 ....51 E4
YEON * BA21 ....35 G4
Charlton Field La SHER DT9 ....19 E1
Chatsworth Rd YEON BA21 ....35 G2
Cheap St SHER DT9 ....39 E3
Chelston Av YEON BA21 ....3 J1
Cherry La RYEO BA22 ....32 C5
Cherry Pie La RYEO BA22 ....4 C4
Cherry Tree Ct CREWK TA18 ....50 D1
Cherry Tree Dr YEOS BA20 ....42 A4
Chessels Cl RYEO BA22 ....41 F5
Chestnut Dr RYEO BA22 ....42 C1
Chestnut Rd MRTK TA12 ....20 B2
Chilthornehill La RYEO BA22 ....23 E3
Chilton Gv YEON BA21 ....34 D3
Chinnock Hollow RYEO BA22 ....40 A5
Chowins Rd CREWK TA18 ....50 D4
Christchurch Rw
CREWK * TA18 ....50 D3
Christopher Cl YEOS BA20 ....2 B3
Chubbs Lawn CREWK * TA18 ....50 D3
Church Cl MRTK TA12 ....20 B3
SHER DT9 ....49 E3
Church Hl RYEO BA22 ....11 F2
Church La RYEO BA22 ....17 G3
RYEO BA22 ....43 E4
SSH TA14 ....30 D5
Church Pth CREWK TA18 ....50 C5
RYEO BA22 ....9 G2
RYEO BA22 ....10 A2
YEOS BA20 ....3 G3
Church Rd RYEO BA22 ....4 C4
RYEO BA22 ....5 H4
SHER DT9 ....44 C3
SHER DT9 ....45 F5

Church St CREWK TA18 ....50 C3
MRTK TA12 ....20 B4
RYEO BA22 ....7 G2
RYEO BA22 ....13 F1
RYEO BA22 ....14 B2
RYEO BA22 ....22 A2
RYEO BA22 ....41 E4
SHER DT9 ....48 D5
YEOS BA20 ....3 G4
Church Ter YEOS * BA20 ....3 G4
Church Wk RYEO BA22 ....16 D2
Churchwell Cl SHER * DT9 ....44 C3
Churchwell St SHER DT9 ....44 C3
Churlands Cl RYEO BA22 ....40 D4
Chur La RYEO BA22 ....41 E5
Clammer Hill La CREWK TA18 ....51 E3
Clanfield SHER DT9 ....38 C5
Clarence St YEOS BA20 ....3 F4
Clarence Ter YEOS BA20 ....3 H5
Clarks Cl RYEO BA22 ....33 F4
Clatcombe La SHER DT9 ....28 D3
Claypits La SHER DT9 ....49 G3
Clayton Cl RYEO BA22 ....33 F3
The Cleve YEON BA21 ....33 H3
Cleaveside Cl RYEO BA22 ....9 H2
Clifton Cl YEON BA21 ....35 H3
Clifton Hl RYEO BA22 ....43 H4
Clifton Rd RYEO BA22 ....44 A4
Clifton Vw RYEO BA22 ....43 F5
The Close RYEO BA22 ....5 H1
Clovermead SHER DT9 ....48 D5
Coat Rd MRTK TA12 ....20 A1
Coker Crs RYEO * BA22 ....41 E5
Coker Hl RYEO BA22 ....40 B5
Cold Harbour SHER DT9 ....39 E2
Cole La SSH TA14 ....30 D1
Coles La SHER DT9 ....48 C4
Collarway La RYEO BA22 ....40 B4
College RYEO BA22 ....40 A5
College Gn YEON BA21 ....3 G1
Colmer Rd YEON BA21 ....35 H3
Combe Pk YEON BA21 ....34 C2
Common La SHER DT9 ....48 B5
Compton Cl YEON BA21 ....35 H1
Compton Rd RYEO BA22 ....5 H5
YEON BA21 ....36 A4
Coniston Gdns YEON BA21 ....34 C2
Constable Cl YEON BA21 ....35 G1
Cooks La SHER DT9 ....39 E4
Coombe La SHER DT9 ....38 D2
Coombe La SHER DT9 ....34 D1
Coombe La SHER DT9 ....28 A5
Coombe Street La YEON BA21 ....34 D1
Coppice Cl YEOS BA20 ....42 A2
Coppits Hill La YEON BA21 ....24 A5
Copse Rd RYEO BA22 ....33 G2
Cornhill SHER DT9 ....38 D3
Coronation Av YEON BA21 ....34 B2
Corton Cl RYEO BA22 ....35 H1
Coryate Cl RYEO BA22 ....40 C1
Cossins La CREWK TA18 ....50 C3
Costello Hl RYEO BA22 ....6 C5
Court Ash YEOS BA20 ....3 G4
Court Barton CREWK TA18 ....50 C3
Court Gdns RYEO BA22 ....17 E2
YEON BA21 ....34 B1
Court La RYEO BA22 ....43 F4
Coverdale Ct YEON * BA21 ....2 D2
Cowen Cl CREWK TA18 ....50 D5
Cowpath La SHER DT9 ....19 H1
Coxs Cl RYEO BA22 ....5 H2
Crangs La SHER DT9 ....11 H1
The Crescent YEOS BA20 ....2 E5
The Croft YEOS BA20 ....41 H2
Crofton Av YEON BA21 ....3 H3
Crofton Pk YEON BA21 ....3 H3
Crofton Rd YEON BA21 ....3 H3
Cromwell Rd YEON BA21 ....35 G3
The Cross SHER DT9 ....44 C3
Crossfields SHER DT9 ....37 E2
Cross Rd SHER DT9 ....44 C2
Culvers Cl SHER DT9 ....38 D3
Curriott Hl CREWK TA18 ....50 B5
Curriott Hill Rd CREWK TA18 ....50 B5
Cutty La RYEO BA22 ....5 H4
Cypress Dr YEOS BA20 ....42 A2

D

Dalwoods *SHER* DT9 ...39 E4
Dampier Pl *YEON* * BA21 ...3 J4
Dampier St *YEOS* BA20 ...3 J4
Danielsfield Rd *YEOS* BA20...42 C2
Dark La *SHER* DT9 ...18 A5
Demelza Ct *RYEO* BA22...9 E2
Denzil Cl *RYEO* BA22...41 E4
Derwent Gdns *YEON* BA21...35 G3
Derwent Wy *YEON* BA21...33 H3
Dibbles La *RYEO* BA22...41 E4
Digby Rd *SHER* DT9...39 E4
Donne La *RYEO* BA22...32 C5
Dorchester Rd *YEOS* BA20...42 D2
Down La *SHER* DT9...26 D4
Downleaze *YEOS* * BA20...42 A2
Dragonfly Cha *RYEO* BA22...6 B4
Dray Rd *RYEO* BA22...40 C1
The Drove *SHER* DT9...45 F4
Droveway La *YEON* BA21...25 G1
Duck La *RYEO* BA22...14 A2
Durrant Cl *SHER* DT9...39 E4

E

Eagle Cl *RYEO* BA22...6 B4
Earle St *YEOS* BA20...3 J5
Earls Cl *SHER* DT9...39 F2
East Coker Rd *YEOS* BA20...42 C3
Eastfield *MRTK* TA12...20 C3
  SHER DT9...45 C5
Easthams Rd *CREWK* TA18...51 E3
Eastland Rd *YEON* BA21...3 J3
Eastlands *SHER* DT9...49 E4
East Mill La *SHER* DT9...39 F3
East Stoke *SSH* TA14...31 F2
East St *CREWK* TA18...50 C3
  MRTK TA12...20 C3
  RYEO BA22...41 E5
Eastville *YEON* BA21...3 K3
Edmond's HI *RYEO* BA22...6 A1
Edward Cl *RYEO* BA22...33 C3
Elborough La *RYEO* BA22...13 H3
Eliotts Dr *YEON* BA21...34 B2
Elmhurst Av *YEON* BA21...35 F3
Elmleigh Rd *MRTK* TA12...20 A3
Englands La *RYEO* BA22...9 H2
Englands Md *RYEO* BA22...9 H2
Ermine St *YEON* BA21...34 A2
Esmonde Dr *RYEO* BA22...6 B4
Everretts *SHER* * DT9...48 D5
Everton Rd *YEOS* BA20...3 F6
Evesham Av *YEON* BA21...33 H3

F

Fairfield *CREWK* TA18...50 C4
  MRTK TA12...20 B2
  SHER DT9...39 E2
Fairhouse Rd *RYEO* BA22...43 F5
Fairmead Rd *YEON* BA21...35 F1
Fairway Vw *YEON* BA21...35 G3
Farm Rd *SHER* DT9...44 B2
Farm St *RYEO* BA22...22 B2
Fennel Wy *RYEO* BA22...33 F4
Ferndale Gdns *YEON* BA21...2 A2
Fernery Rd *YEON* BA21...3 A2
Fiddle La *RYEO* BA22...16 D2
Fielding Rd *YEON* BA21...3 J2
Fishers Cl *SHER* DT9...26 D4
Flaxfield Dr *CREWK* TA18...50 D4
Flax La *SHER* DT9...37 E2
Flax Wy *YEON* BA21...33 H3
Flushing Meadow *YEON* BA21...35 H4
Foldhill Cl *MRTK* TA12...20 C3
Foldhill La *MRTK* TA12...20 C3
Folly Flds *YEON* BA21...35 E2
Folly La *RYEO* BA22...5 H5
  SHER DT9...37 E1
Font La *RYEO* BA22...41 F5
Font Vls *RYEO* BA22...41 F5
Forde Pk *RYEO* BA22...33 C2
Forest HI *YEOS* BA20...42 B1
Fore St *RYEO* BA22...9 E2
Forts Orch *RYEO* BA22...23 C3
Fosse Cl *YEON* BA21...34 A2
Fosse Wy *YEON* BA21...34 A2
Fosters *SHER* DT9...39 F3
Foundry Sq *CREWK* TA18...50 D4
Foxcote *YEOS* * BA20...41 H2
Foxglove Wy *RYEO* BA22...33 F4

Fox Mdw *CREWK* TA18...51 E2
Frederick Pl *YEOS* * BA20...3 H4
Freedom Av *YEON* BA21...2 A1
Free St *SHER* DT9...13 F1
Friars Av *YEON* BA21...34 A3
Friars Cl *RYEO* BA22...13 E1
Frog La *RYEO* BA22...8 D2
Furland Rd *CREWK* TA18...50 D4
The Furlongs *SHER* DT9...39 E2
The Furze *YEOS* BA20...41 H2

G

Gainsborough Dr *SHER* DT9...38 B4
Gainsborough HI *SHER* DT9...39 F5
Gainsborough Wy *YEON* BA21...35 H1
The Gardens *SHER* * DT9...38 D4
Garrett Rd *YEOS* BA20...42 A1
Garston La *RYEO* BA22...16 D2
Gason La *RYEO* BA22...9 H1
Gazelle Rd *YEOS* BA20...42 A1
George La *CREWK* * TA18...50 D3
George St *SHER* DT9...39 E3
Gifle Vw *SHER* DT9...45 F4
Glastonbury Ct *YEON* BA21...34 A3
The Glebe *RYEO* BA22...9 H2
Glebe Cl *SHER* DT9...45 F5
Glebelands *SSH* TA14...30 D5
Glenthorne Av *YEON* BA21...35 E2
Glenville Rd *YEON* BA21...35 G3
Glovers Cl *SSH* TA14...30 D1
Glovers Wk *YEOS* BA20...3 H5
Goldcroft *YEON* BA21...3 G1
Gooseacre La *RYEO* BA22...41 F4
Gooseland La *SHER* DT9...37 H3
Gordon Rd *YEON* BA21...3 J2
Gordon's La *SHER* DT9...46 D5
Gouldsbrook Ter *CREWK* TA18...50 C3
Grace Martin's La *RYEO* BA22...10 A2
Grange Pk *SHER* DT9...45 F5
Granville Wy *SHER* DT9...39 F2
Grass Royal *YEON* BA21...3 K2
Great Cnr *YEON* * BA21...33 H5
Great Field La *SSH* TA14...30 D2
Great Orch *RYEO* BA22...6 B5
Great Pit La *RYEO* BA22...27 C1
Great St *SSH* TA14...30 C5
Great Western Rd *MRTK* TA12...20 B1
Great Western Ter *YEON* BA21...35 C4
The Green *RYEO* BA22...6 B4
  SHER DT9...39 E3
Greenacres Pk *YEON* * BA21...24 B5
Green Cl *RYEO* BA22...4 C5
Greenhill *SHER* DT9...39 E3
Greenhill Rd *YEON* BA21...35 F2
Green La *RYEO* BA22...9 H2
  RYEO BA22...40 A4
  RYEO BA22...41 C4
Green Md *RYEO* BA22...33 H3
Greenmoor La *YEON* BA21...24 C4
Greenwood Rd *YEON* BA21...34 A2
Grove Av *YEOS* BA20...3 D5
Guard Av *YEOS* BA20...33 G3
Guinevere Cl *YEON* BA21...34 A2
Gunners La *RYEO* BA22...33 F4
Gunville La *RYEO* BA22...42 B4

H

Hales Meadow *YEON* BA21...25 H3
Half Acres *SHER* DT9...38 D4
Half Moon St *SHER* DT9...39 E4
Hallet Gdns *YEOS* BA20...2 E5
Halletts Orch *RYEO* BA22...22 A3
Halves La *RYEO* BA22...41 F5
Hamdon Cl *SSH* TA14...30 D2
Hamdon Vw *SSH* TA14...30 C4
Ham Hill Rd *RYEO* BA22...32 B5
  SSH TA14...30 D2
Ham La *SHER* DT9...27 E4
Hampton Cl *RYEO* BA22...43 G4
Harbour *YEON* * BA21...33 H4
Harbour Rd *SHER* DT9...39 F2
Harbour Wy *SHER* DT9...39 E2
Hardy Ct *CREWK* TA18...50 D4
Harper Rd *CREWK* TA18...50 D4
Hart's La *SHER* DT9...37 G3
Hathermead Gdns *YEON* BA21...35 G3
Hawkins Wy *YEON* BA21...33 H3
Hawthorne Cl *CREWK* TA18...51 E6
Hawthorn Rd *YEON* BA21...35 G2
Hazel Vw *CREWK* TA18...51 E2
Head St *RYEO* BA22...22 A3
Heathcote Rd *RYEO* BA22...7 F4

Heather Rd *YEON* BA21...35 F2
Heather Wy *RYEO* BA22...33 F4
Helena Rd *YEOS* BA20...42 A3
Hendford *YEOS* BA20...3 F6
Hendford Gv *YEOS* BA20...3 F5
Hendford HI *YEOS* BA20...42 C1
Henhayes La *CREWK* TA18...50 D3
Henley Vw *CREWK* TA18...50 D5
Herblay Cl *YEON* BA21...35 H3
Hermes Pl *RYEO* BA22...6 B4
Hermitage St *CREWK* TA18...50 D4
Hertford Rd *YEON* BA21...35 H1
Hewish La *CREWK* TA18...50 B1
Higher Bullen *RYEO* BA22...43 F5
Higher Cheap St *SHER* DT9...39 E3
Higher Easthams La *CREWK* TA18...51 F2
Higher Kingston *YEOS* BA20...3 F3
Higher Ream *YEON* BA21...33 H3
Higher St *MRTK* TA12...30 A1
  SSH TA14...30 C5
Higher Westbury *SHER* DT9...44 C3
Highfield *RYEO* BA22...3 J1
Highfield Ter *MRTK* TA12...20 A5
High Lea *YEON* BA21...35 E1
Highmore Rd *SHER* DT9...38 D2
High St *RYEO* BA22...4 B4
  RYEO BA22...5 H2
  RYEO BA22...10 A2
  RYEO BA22...13 F1
  RYEO BA22...17 G3
  RYEO BA22...40 A5
  RYEO BA22...41 E4
  SHER DT9...48 D5
  SSH TA14...31 E2
  YEOS BA20...3 G5
Highwoods Cl *SSH* TA14...30 D5
Hillborne Gdns *YEON* BA21...33 H4
Hill Brow *SHER* DT9...38 C5
Hill Crest Rd *YEON* BA21...3 J1
Hillgrove Av *YEOS* BA20...42 C2
Hill House Cl *SHER* DT9...39 F2
Hillingdon Ct *YEON* BA21...33 H3
Hillside Ter *YEON* BA21...3 K3
Hillside Vw *RYEO* BA22...43 G4
Hill's La *MRTK* TA12...20 B2
Hills Orch *MRTK* TA12...20 B2
Hill Vw *YEOS* BA20...3 K4
Hill View Cl *SSH* TA14...30 C2
Hinton Rd *CREWK* TA18...50 C2
The Hollies *CREWK* TA18...50 D5
  YEON BA21...35 F2
Hollow La *MCUTE* TA15...31 H4
Holly Gv *CREWK* TA18...51 E2
Holly Tree Wk *YEOS* BA20...42 B1
Home Dr *YEON* BA21...2 A2
Home Farm La *RYEO* BA22...17 F3
Honeycombe Ri *SHER* DT9...38 B5
Hook Dro *RYEO* BA22...14 D2
Horncastles La *SHER* DT9...38 D4
Horsecastles *SHER* DT9...38 D4
Horsecastles La *SHER* DT9...38 C3
Horsey La *YEOS* BA20...2 E6
Horton Cl *YEON* BA21...34 A3
Hospital La *SHER* DT9...39 E3
Houndstone Cl *YEON* BA21...33 H4
Houndstone Ct *RYEO* BA22...33 F4
Hound St *SHER* DT9...39 E3
Howard Rd *YEON* BA21...35 H3
Howell HI *RYEO* BA22...9 E1
Huish *YEOS* BA20...2 D5
Huish Gdns *YEOS* BA20...2 E4
Hundredstone Cl *YEON* BA21...35 E1
Hunts Md *SHER* DT9...38 C5
Hurst *MRTK* TA12...20 A4
Hurst Pk *MRTK* TA12...20 A4
Hyde Ct *YEON* BA21...33 H3
Hyde Rd *MCUTE* TA15...31 H2

I

Ilchester Rd *YEON* BA21...23 H3
  YEON BA21...34 C2
Illustrious Crs *RYEO* BA22...6 B4
Ivel Ct *YEOS* BA20...3 J4
Ivel Gdns *RYEO* BA22...13 F1
Ivel Sq *YEOS* BA20...3 H4
Ivelway *CREWK* TA18...50 D4
Ivy Wk *YEOS* BA20...42 B1

J

Jasmine Cl *CREWK* TA18...51 E2
  RYEO BA22...33 G4
Jubilee Pl *YEON* * BA21...34 A4

Juniper Cl *YEOS* BA20...42

K

Keep St *RYEO* BA22...8
Kember's HI *RYEO* BA22...11
Kenmore Dr *YEON* BA21...3
Kiddles *YEON* BA21...3
King Arthur Dr *YEON* BA21...34
King George St *YEOS* BA20...3
Kings Cl *SHER* DT9...47
Kings Crs *SHER* DT9...39
Kingshams *RYEO* BA22...13
Kings HI *RYEO* BA22...23
Kings Rd *SHER* DT9...49
  SHER DT9...49
  SSH TA14...20
Kingston *YEOS* BA20...3
Kingston Vw *YEON* BA21...3
King St *YEON* BA21...3
Kingswood Rd *CREWK* TA18...50
Kithill *CREWK* TA18...50
Kitt HI *SHER* DT9...38
Knotts Paddock *SHER* DT9...39

L

Laburnum Crs *CREWK* TA18...51
Laburnum Wy *YEOS* BA20...42
Lakefields *RYEO* BA22...41
Lambourne Ct *CREWK* TA18...51
Lambsfield *RYEO* BA22...39
Landshire La *RYEO* BA22...40
Langdons *SHER* DT9...39
Langlands *SSH* TA14...
Langmead Pl *CREWK* TA18...50
Langmead Rd *CREWK* TA18...50
Langmead Sq *CREWK* TA18...50
Lang Rd *CREWK* TA18...50
Larkhill Rd *YEON* BA21...23
Larkspur Crs *YEON* BA21...34
Laurel Cl *RYEO* BA22...41
Laurel La *RYEO* BA22...9
The Laurels *CREWK* TA18...50
Lavers Oak *MRTK* TA12...20
Lawson Cl *MRTK* TA12...20
Lea Cl *YEON* BA21...35
Leaze La *YEON* BA21...35
Leet Ct *SHER* DT9...38
Legion Rd *YEON* BA21...2
Leland Trail *RYEO* BA22...8
  RYEO BA22...14
  SSH TA14...30
Leland Trail & Monarch's Wy
  RYEO BA22...12
Lenthay Cl *SHER* DT9...38
Lenthay Rd *SHER* DT9...38
Liberty Trail *SSH* TA14...31
Limber Rd *RYEO* BA22...33
Limbury *MRTK* TA12...20
Lime Kiln *YEON* BA21...33
Lime Tree Av *YEOS* BA20...42
Limington Rd *RYEO* BA22...13
Linden Rd *YEOS* BA20...2
Lingfield Av *YEON* BA21...35
Littlefield *SHER* DT9...38
Little Marston Rd *RYEO* BA22...16
Little Md *SSH* TA14...30
Little Meadow *RYEO* BA22...6
Little Orchards *MRTK* TA12...20
Little Sammons *RYEO* BA22...23
Little St *SSH* TA14...30
Little Trumps *RYEO* BA22...20
London Sq *MRTK* TA12...20
Long Cl *YEON* BA21...33
Longcroft Rd *YEON* BA21...3
Longdown Rd *SHER* DT9...49
Longford Rd *SHER* DT9...49
Long Furlong La *RYEO* BA22...41
Longlands La *RYEO* BA22...40
Long Md *RYEO* BA22...33
Long Run *RYEO* BA22...40
Long St *SHER* DT9...39
Lower Acreman St *SHER* DT9...39
Lower Boynston La *SHER* DT9...29
Lower East Coker Rd
  YEOS BA20...42
Lower Fairmead Rd *YEON* BA21...35
Lower Hyde Rd *MCUTE* TA15...31
Lower Odcombe *RYEO* BA22...32
Lower Ream *YEON* BA21...33
Lower Turners Barn La
  YEOS BA20...42
Lower Wraxhill Rd *YEOS* BA20...42

's Hill La SHER DT9 37 H4
ther Rd YEON BA21 35 H2
bourne Rd SHER DT9 39 F4
on Wy RYEO BA22 33 G3
e La YEON BA21 36 A3
e Rd YEON BA21 25 G5
water CREWK TA18 50 C3
ie Rd CREWK TA18 50 C5
dhurst Gv MRTK TA12 20 A1
ander Rd YEOS BA20 42 A1
er Cl RYEO BA22 13 F2

M

cmillan Wy SHER DT9 28 D2
HER * DT9 39 E4
HER DT9 49 F5
gna Cl YEON BA21 35 G1
ncombe Cl CREWK TA18 50 C5
n St RYEO BA22 23 F4
mesbury Wy RYEO BA22 33 H3
thouse La SHER DT9 27 E4
Maltings SHER * DT9 39 F3
vern Ct YEON BA21 34 A3
nor Cl RYEO BA22 4 C5
HER DT9 44 B2
nor Ct SHER * DT9 39 E3
nor Dr RYEO BA22 41 F5
nor Farm RYEO BA22 41 E4
nor Gdns RYEO BA22 13 F1
nor Rd YEOS BA20 3 F6
nor St RYEO BA22 41 E5
nor Vw CREWK TA18 50 D5
ple Dr CREWK TA18 51 E2
EOS BA20 42 C1
rket Pl RYEO BA22 13 F1
rket Sq CREWK TA18 50 C3
rket St CREWK TA18 50 D3
EOS BA20 3 H4
rlborough Rd YEON BA21 35 H3
rl Cl YEON BA21 34 B2
rl La SHER DT9 36 C3
rsh La RYEO BA22 21 H3
SH TA14 31 G1
EON BA21 24 C5
rston Rd SHER DT9 38 B1
rtock La MRTK TA12 20 D2
rwin Cl MRTK TA12 20 B1
ry St YEON BA21 3 H3
son La MCUTE TA15 31 H2
tfurlong Cl MRTK TA12 20 A4
tthews Rd YEON BA21 3 K3
tt's La SSH TA14 30 D2
yfield Rd YEON BA21 35 G3
Creery Rd SHER DT9 39 E1
ad Av RYEO BA22 33 G3
adow Rd YEON BA21 35 G2
adow Vw RYEO BA22 41 H5
YEO BA22 43 G4
lbury Rd SHER DT9 48 D5
lrose Rd YEON BA21 3 H1
morial Av CREWK TA18 50 D4
morial Rd RYEO BA22 33 G3
ddle Field La SHER DT9 28 A1
ddle Pth CREWK TA18 50 C3
ddle Ridge La SHER DT9 18 D2
ddle St MCUTE TA15 32 A3
YEO BA22 17 G3
EOS BA20 3 H5
dleaze SHER DT9 38 B4
dmay Dr RYEO BA22 10 A2
ford Pk YEON BA21 35 E2
ford Rd YEON BA21 3 H1
lbrook YEOS BA20 2 E6
l Cl RYEO BA22 42 A5
lfield RYEO BA22 6 C4
l La CREWK TA18 51 E5
CREWK TA18 51 H5
RYEO BA22 14 A2
RYEO BA22 41 G5
SHER DT9 26 D5
SHER DT9 44 C3
YEOS BA20 3 H5
l St RYEO BA22 17 G2
ton Cl YEON BA21 33 H3
nchington's Cl SSH TA14 30 D5
tchells Rw RYEO * BA22 5 H1
tchelmore Rd YEON BA21 3 G2
narch's Wy RYEO BA22 14 B2
RYEO BA22 22 D1
SHER DT9 18 D5
SHER DT9 27 G5
SSH TA14 31 F3
YEOS BA20 3 K4
narch's Wy & Macmillan Wy
SHER DT9 18 C4

Monks Dl YEON BA21 34 A4
Monmouth Rd YEON BA21 35 G2
Montacute Rd RYEO BA22 22 A3
SSH TA14 31 H2
Montrose Rd YEON BA21 35 H2
Moorlands Cl MRTK TA12 20 B2
Moorlands Pk MRTK TA12 20 B3
Moorway La SHER DT9 28 A2
Morston SHER DT9 45 G5
Mount Pleasant CREWK TA18 51 E3
YEON BA21 3 J3
Movey La RYEO BA22 14 A2
Mow Barton MRTK TA12 20 B2
Mowleaze RYEO BA22 43 F4
Muchelney Wy RYEO BA22 33 G2
Mudford Hl YEON BA21 25 G5
Mudford Rd YEON BA21 3 F1
Mulberry Gdns CREWK TA18 50 D4
Mulberry La SSH TA14 31 F1
Murray-Smith Dr RYEO BA22 33 F3
Musmoor La RYEO BA22 4 A1
Myrtle Rd MRTK TA12 20 B3

N

Nash La YEOS BA20 42 A3
Nathan Cl YEOS BA20 42 A2
Neathem Rd YEON BA21 35 F2
Nethercoombe La SHER DT9 38 D2
Netherton La RYEO BA22 17 F2
Netherton Rd YEON BA21 35 G2
Netley YEON BA21 34 A3
Newbury Ter YEON BA21 34 C2
Newcross SHER DT9 47 G5
Newell SHER DT9 38 D3
Newland SHER DT9 39 E3
Newland Gdn SHER DT9 39 F3
New Rd RYEO BA22 32 D4
RYEO BA22 43 F5
SHER DT9 39 E5
SSH TA14 30 C4
Newton Rd RYEO BA22 43 G4
YEOS BA20 3 K6
Nightingale La RYEO BA22 4 A1
Noake Rd SHER DT9 38 C4
Northbrook Rd YEON BA21 35 F2
Northern Wy CREWK * TA18 50 D3
North La YEOS BA20 3 G4
North Rd SHER DT9 39 F2
North St CREWK TA18 50 D2
MRTK TA12 20 B2
SHER DT9 44 C2
SSH TA14 20 D5
North Ter YEON BA21 3 J2
Norton Rd SSH TA14 30 C3
Nursery Rd YEOS BA20 2 E7

O

Oakland Dr MRTK TA12 20 B1
Oakland Rd MRTK TA12 20 B1
Oaklands Rd YEON BA21 35 G2
Oakleigh YEOS BA20 42 A2
Oakley La RYEO BA22 23 H2
Oakridge Pk YEON * BA21 2 E2
Oak Wy RYEO BA22 33 F2
Oborne Rd SHER DT9 39 G2
Odcombe Hollow RYEO BA22 40 A5
Old Barn Wy YEOS BA20 42 B2
Old Market MRTK TA12 20 B2
Old Rd RYEO BA22 40 C1
Old Station Rd YEOS BA20 3 J5
Orchard Barn SSH TA14 30 C4
Orchard Cl RYEO BA22 4 C4
RYEO BA22 40 C1
RYEO BA22 41 E5
YEON BA21 24 B4
Orchard La CREWK TA18 50 D3
Orchard Pl RYEO BA22 10 A2
Orchard Ri CREWK TA18 50 D4
Orchard St YEOS BA20 2 D5
Osborne Rd YEOS BA20 2 E4
Ottery La SHER DT9 38 D4
Oxen Rd CREWK TA18 50 D3
Oxford Rd YEON BA21 36 A2

P

The Paddocks RYEO BA22 13 F2
SHER DT9 45 F4
Pageant Dr SHER DT9 39 E4
Parcroft Gdns YEOS BA20 2 D3

Parfields YEOS BA20 2 C4
Parish Hl RYEO BA22 5 H3
The Park YEOS BA20 2 E3
Park Gdns YEOS BA20 3 F4
Park La RYEO BA22 32 A4
Park Rd YEOS BA20 3 F4
Park St YEOS BA20 3 G7
Park Vw CREWK TA18 50 D5
MCUTE TA15 32 A3
Parsonage Rd RYEO BA22 9 E2
Patson Hill La SHER DT9 27 H4
Pattinson Cl YEON BA21 35 G3
Pavyotts La RYEO BA22 42 D4
Pembroke Cl YEON BA21 35 H2
Penmore Rd SHER DT9 27 G2
Penn Hl YEOS BA20 3 G6
Penn Hill Pk YEOS BA20 3 G6
Percy Rd YEON BA21 35 G3
Peter St YEOS BA20 3 G5
Petter's Wy YEOS BA20 3 G6
Pettitts Cl SHER DT9 44 B2
Pickett La YEON BA21 34 D2
Pill Bridge La RYEO BA22 12 D1
Pine Tree Av YEOS BA20 42 C1
Pinford La SHER DT9 39 G3
Pink Knoll Hollow SHER DT9 18 A3
Pitfield Cnr RYEO BA22 17 F5
Placket La YEOS BA20 42 A3
Plantagenet Cha YEOS BA20 42 A1
Plantagenet Pk YEOS BA20 42 B1
Plot La SHER DT9 27 E5
Plover Ct YEON BA21 34 A3
Plowage La RYEO BA22 8 D2
Plum Orch SHER DT9 37 E2
Poplar Dr YEON BA21 33 H2
Poplars Cl YEON BA21 24 B4
Pople's Well CREWK TA18 50 C3
Poppy Cl RYEO BA22 33 G4
Portman Ct RYEO BA22 40 A5
Portreeve Dr YEON BA21 3 H2
Pound Cl YEON BA21 33 H4
Pound La MRTK TA12 20 A3
Pound Rd SHER DT9 45 F5
Preston Gv YEOS BA20 2 A3
Preston Rd RYEO BA22 33 F4
Priestlands SHER DT9 39 E2
Priestlands La SHER DT9 39 E3
Primrose La YEON BA21 25 G5
Prince's Cl SSH TA14 30 D2
Princes St YEOS BA20 3 G5
Priory Cl RYEO BA22 13 E1
YEOS BA20 42 A3
Priory Gld YEON BA21 33 H3
Priory Rd RYEO BA22 13 F1
Prophet's La SSH TA14 30 A3
Pulmans La CREWK TA18 50 D4
Putts La SHER DT9 18 D2
SHER DT9 19 E2
Pyle La RYEO BA22 7 G5

Q

Quarr Dr SHER DT9 39 E1
Quarr La SHER DT9 39 E1
Quarr Lane Pk SHER * DT9 39 E1
Quarry La SHER DT9 44 B1
SHER DT9 47 G5
Queens Crs SSH TA14 20 D5
Queens Rd SHER DT9 44 C2
Queens Ter SHER * DT9 39 E2
Queen St RYEO BA22 22 A1
SHER DT9 48 D5
Queensway YEOS BA20 2 E6
Queensway Pl YEOS BA20 3 F5

R

Raglan Ter YEON BA21 34 B2
Ratleigh La SHER DT9 37 G3
Reckleford YEOS BA20 3 G4
Rectory Farm Cl RYEO BA22 9 H3
Rectory Hl RYEO BA22 11 F2
Rectory La RYEO BA22 10 C2
SSH TA14 30 D5
Redgate Pk CREWK TA18 50 D1
Redhole La SHER DT9 28 D4
Redwood Rd YEON BA21 35 H1
The Regents YEON BA21 33 H3
Rex Rd RYEO BA22 40 C1
Rex's La RYEO BA22 43 F4
Rhydderch Wy CREWK TA18 50 D4
Richmond Cl SHER DT9 38 D4
Richmond Gn SHER DT9 38 D4
Richmond Rd SHER DT9 38 D4

YEOS BA20 2 E5
Richmond Wy YEON BA21 33 H3
The Ridge SHER DT9 29 H1
Ridge La RYEO BA22 40 C5
SHER DT9 18 D1
Ridgemead YEOS BA20 42 A2
Ridgeway SHER DT9 38 C4
Ridgeway La RYEO BA22 5 G2
Rigg La SHER DT9 27 E4
Rimpton Hl RYEO BA22 17 F5
Rimpton Rd RYEO BA22 17 E2
Ringwell Hl MRTK TA12 30 A1
Ritchie Rd RYEO BA22 33 F4
River Parrett Trail MRTK TA12 20 A5
River Parrett Trail &
Monarch's Wy CREWK TA18 51 G1
Riverside Wk YEOS BA20 3 K4
Rivers Rd YEON BA21 35 G1
Roe Av RYEO BA22 33 F4
Roe La RYEO BA22 17 G3
Romsey Rd YEON BA21 35 H2
Rope Wk MRTK TA12 20 B2
Roping Rd YEON BA21 3 G2
Rosebery Av YEON BA21 35 G3
Rose La CREWK TA18 50 C3
Rowan Wy YEOS BA20 42 C1
Rowbarrow Hl SHER DT9 27 E2
Ruddock Cl RYEO BA22 41 F5
Ruddock Wy RYEO BA22 41 F5
Runnymede Rd YEON BA21 35 G1
Rush Cl RYEO * BA22 5 H5
Russet Wy YEOS BA20 42 A2
Rustywell Pk YEOS BA20 2 D7
Ryefields Cl RYEO BA22 41 F5
Rye Gdns YEOS BA20 42 A2
Ryme Rd SHER DT9 48 C5

S

St Aldhelm's Rd SHER DT9 39 E1
St Andrews Rd YEOS BA20 2 B3
St Anne's Gdns YEON BA21 2 A1
St Catherine's Crs SHER DT9 38 C4
St David's Crs YEON BA21 35 E2
St George's Av YEON BA21 35 E2
St James's Cl YEON BA21 34 A4
St James's Pk YEON BA21 33 H4
St John's Rd YEON BA21 35 F2
St Leonards Ct YEOS * BA20 2 D5
St Margaret's Rd RYEO BA22 22 A3
St Martins Wy YEOS BA20 42 A2
St Mary's Crs YEON BA21 35 F1
St Mary's Rd SHER DT9 38 C4
St Michael's Av YEON BA21 35 E1
St Michaels Cl SHER DT9 36 D3
St Michael's Rd YEON BA21 35 G3
St Nicholas Cl YEOS BA20 3 G5
St Nicholas Pk YEOS BA20 3 G6
St Osmund Cl SHER DT9 48 D5
St Patrick's Rd YEON BA21 34 A2
St Paul's Cl SHER DT9 39 E1
St Paul's Gn SHER DT9 39 F1
St Swithins Cl SHER DT9 39 F3
St Swithin's Rd SHER DT9 39 F3
St Thomas Cross YEON BA21 3 K3
Salthouse La YEOS BA20 3 F5
Samways Cl RYEO * BA22 33 G4
Sandford Orcas Rd SHER DT9 28 C2
Sandhurst Rd YEOS BA20 42 C2
Sandlewood Cl YEON BA21 35 H1
Sandown Cl YEOS BA20 2 E4
Sandringham Rd YEON BA21 35 H3
Sarum SHER DT9 45 G4
School Cl RYEO BA22 22 B3
Seaborough Vw CREWK TA18 50 D5
Sea King Rd YEOS BA20 42 A1
Seaton Rd YEOS BA20 2 D5
Sedgemoor Cl YEON BA21 35 G2
Severalls Park Av CREWK TA18 50 D4
The Sheeplands SHER DT9 38 C2
Sheeplands La SHER DT9 38 C3
Shelley Cl YEON BA21 34 A3
Sherborne Hl SHER DT9 47 F1
Sherborne Rd YEON BA21 3 K3
Shiller's La SHER DT9 18 B5
Shute Lake La CREWK TA18 51 E4
Silver St RYEO BA22 43 F5
YEOS BA20 3 G5
Simons Rd SHER DT9 39 E2
Skinner's La SSH TA14 30 D5
Slade La RYEO BA22 17 G5
Sleight Cl YEON BA21 33 H3
Slow Court La RYEO BA22 8 D2
Smith's Ter YEON BA21 3 J2
Sock Hl YEON BA21 25 G3
Sock La RYEO BA22 25 E3

Somerset Pl *YEOS* BA20 ....3 F7
South Av *SHER* DT9 ....38 C5
Southcombe Wy *RYEO* BA22 ....22 A3
South Ct *SHER* DT9 ....38 C4
Southmead *RYEO* BA22 ....8 D3
Southmead Crs *CREWK* TA18 ....50 D4
South St *CREWK* TA18 ....51 E4
MCUTE TA15 ....32 A3
RYEO BA22 ....8 D2
SHER DT9 ....39 E4
YEOS BA20 ....3 H5
South Vw *RYEO* * BA22 ....9 H3
SHER DT9 ....44 C2
Southville *YEON* BA21 ....3 J3
Southway Cl *YEON* BA21 ....2 D1
Southway Crs *YEON* BA21 ....2 D1
Southway Dr *YEON* BA21 ....2 D1
South Western Ter *YEOS* BA20 ....3 J5
Southwoods *YEOS* BA20 ....42 D1
Sparkford Hill La *RYEO* BA22 ....10 A1
Sparkford Rd *RYEO* BA22 ....4 B1
Sparrow Rd *YEON* BA21 ....3 F2
Speckington La *RYEO* BA22 ....8 A4
The Spinney *YEOS* BA20 ....42 A2
Springfield Crs *SHER* DT9 ....38 D4
Springfield Pl *YEON* BA21 ....34 B2
Springfield Rd *YEON* BA21 ....34 B2
Spring La *SHER* DT9 ....28 C1
Stapleton Cl *MRTK* TA12 ....20 B1
Stapleton Rd *MRTK* TA12 ....20 B1
Stars La *YEOS* BA20 ....3 H5
Station Rd *CREWK* TA18 ....51 F5
SHER DT9 ....39 E4
Steppes Crs *MRTK* TA12 ....20 B2
Steppes Meadow *MRTK* TA12 ....20 B2
Stiby Rd *YEON* BA21 ....34 C2
Stoke Rd *MRTK* TA12 ....20 B4
Stonedene *SHER* DT9 ....39 E1
Stonehill *SHER* DT9 ....11 G3
SSH TA14 ....31 F2
Stone La *YEON* BA21 ....34 D1
Stonyacres *SHER* DT9 ....48 D4
Stourton Wy *YEON* BA21 ....33 H3
Stratford La *YEON* BA21 ....34 A4
Stratford Rd *YEON* BA21 ....34 A4
Street La *RYEO* BA22 ....40 A2
Summerhouse Ter *YEOS* BA20 ....3 H6
Summerhouse Vw *YEON* BA21 ....3 J2
Summerlands *YEON* BA21 ....2 B2
Summerleaze Pk *YEOS* BA20 ....2 C3
Sunningdale Rd *YEON* BA21 ....3 K1
Sussex Farm Wy *SHER* DT9 ....49 E5
Sutton Gra *YEON* BA21 ....33 H3
Swallowcliffe Gdns *YEOS* BA20 ....3 F3
Sycamore Dr *CREWK* TA18 ....51 E2
YEOS BA20 ....42 C2
Sydling Rd *YEON* BA21 ....35 G3

T

Tabernacle La *YEOS* BA20 ....3 G5
Tannery Ct *CREWK* * TA18 ....50 D2
Taranto Hl *RYEO* BA22 ....6 B4
Taranto Wy *RYEO* BA22 ....7 G4
Tarratt La *YEOS* BA20 ....42 D3
Tarratt Rd *YEOS* BA20 ....42 C3
Termare Cl *RYEO* BA22 ....33 G3
The Terrace *SHER* * DT9 ....45 F5
Terrace Vw *SHER* * DT9 ....38 D4
SHER * DT9 ....39 F2
Tewkesbury *YEON* BA21 ....34 A3
Thatcham Cl *YEON* BA21 ....34 C2
Thatcham Ct *YEON* BA21 ....34 C2
Thatcham Pk *YEON* BA21 ....34 C2
Thatcham Park Cl *YEON* BA21 ....34 C2
Thomson Dr *CREWK* TA18 ....51 E4
Thorne Gdns *YEON* BA21 ....33 H2
Thorne La *YEON* BA21 ....33 G2
YEON BA21 ....34 B1
Thornford Rd *SHER* DT9 ....48 D3
Thornhill La *RYEO* BA22 ....14 B3
Thornton Rd *YEON* BA21 ....34 A2
Thorny La *RYEO* BA22 ....16 C3
SHER DT9 ....26 C2
Three Corner Md *YEON* BA21 ....33 H4
Thurlocks *RYEO* BA22 ....22 A3
Tinneys La *SHER* DT9 ....39 F3
Tintagel Rd *YEON* BA21 ....33 H1
Tintern *YEON* BA21 ....33 H3
Tintinhull Rd *YEON* BA21 ....23 G5
Tiptoft *SSH* TA14 ....30 D1
The Toose *YEON* BA21 ....33 H3
The Torre *YEON* BA21 ....33 H3
Tower Hill Rd *CREWK* TA18 ....50 C4
Tower Rd *YEON* BA21 ....35 F1
Townsend *MCUTE* TA15 ....32 A3
RYEO BA22 ....16 C2
Traits La *RYEO* BA22 ....9 G1
Trellech Ct *RYEO* BA22 ....33 H3
Trendle St *SHER* DT9 ....39 E4
Trent Cl *YEON* BA21 ....35 H1
Trent Path La *SHER* DT9 ....38 B2
Tresco Spinney *YEON* BA21 ....33 H3
Trill La *RYEO* BA22 ....48 C1
Tuncombe La *CREWK* TA18 ....50 A3
Tunwell La *SSH* TA14 ....30 D1
Turner's Barn La *YEOS* BA20 ....42 C2
Twines Cl *RYEO* BA22 ....4 C5
Two Elms *RYEO* BA22 ....16 B3
Two Tower La *YEOS* BA20 ....42 D2

U

Underdown Hollow *SHER* DT9 ....44 A1
Union St *YEOS* BA20 ....3 G5
Uplands *SHER* DT9 ....48 D5

V

Vagg La *YEON* BA21 ....23 H3
Vale Cl *CREWK* TA18 ....50 D5
Vale Rd *YEON* BA21 ....35 H3
Valley Cl *YEON* BA21 ....3 H2
Valley Rd *CREWK* TA18 ....50 D5
Vernalls Rd *SHER* DT9 ....39 E2
Vicarage St *RYEO* BA22 ....22 A2
YEOS BA20 ....3 H5
Victoria Cl *YEON* BA21 ....35 G3
Victoria Rd *YEON* BA21 ....35 G3
Vincent Pl *YEOS* BA20 ....3 H4
Vincent St *YEOS* * BA20 ....3 H4
Vixen Cl *RYEO* BA22 ....7 G3

W

The Waldrons *SHER* DT9 ....45 G5
Wales La *RYEO* BA22 ....9 G2
Walscombe Cl *SSH* TA14 ....30 D1
Wash La *MCUTE* TA15 ....32 A3
Watercombe Hts *YEOS* BA20 ....42 A2
Watercombe La *YEOS* BA20 ....41 H2
Watercombe Pk *YEOS* BA20 ....42 A1
Water St *MRTK* TA12 ....20 A4
Watling St *YEON* BA21 ....34 A2
Waygranville *SHER* DT9 ....39 F1
Weavers Cl *CREWK* TA18 ....51 E4
Weir La *RYEO* BA22 ....14 B1
Welbeck Rd *YEON* BA21 ....35 G2
Welland Rd *YEON* BA21 ....35 G2
Wentworth Rd *YEON* BA21 ....35 H2
Wessex Dr *SHER* DT9 ....44 C3
Wessex Rd *YEON* BA21 ....34 A1
Westbourne Cl *YEOS* BA20 ....2 B4
Westbourne Gv *YEOS* BA20 ....2 A4
Westbridge Pk *SHER* DT9 ....38 C5
West Brook *YEON* BA21 ....34 A3
Westbury *SHER* DT9 ....39 E5
SHER DT9 ....44 C2
Westbury Gdns *RYEO* BA22 ....40 B1
West Camel Farm *RYEO* BA22 ....9 E2
West Camel Rd *RYEO* BA22 ....9 F3
West Coker Rd *YEOS* BA20 ....41 H3
West Coombe *YEON* * BA21 ....34 A3
Western Av *YEON* BA21 ....33 G2
Western St *SHER* DT9 ....36 C2
Westfield *SHER* DT9 ....38 C5
Westfield Av *YEON* BA21 ....2 B1
Westfield Crs *YEON* BA21 ....2 C1
Westfield Gv *YEON* BA21 ....2 D1
Westfield Pl *YEON* BA21 ....2 B1
Westfield Rd *YEON* BA21 ....2 C1
West Hendford *YEOS* BA20 ....2 D7
Westland Rd *YEOS* BA20 ....2 C6
West Mill La *SHER* DT9 ....46 D1
Westminster *RYEO* BA22 ....33 G3
Westminster St *YEOS* BA20 ....3 F5
West Pk *YEOS* BA20 ....2 D3
Westridge *SHER* DT9 ....38 D4
West St *CREWK* TA18 ....50 C3
RYEO BA22 ....13 F2
SSH TA14 ....30 B3
YEOS BA20 ....2 D5
West Ter *SHER* * DT9 ....39 E4
Westville *YEON* BA21 ....3 J3
Whellers Meadow *MRTK* TA12 20
Whirligig La *SSH* TA14 30
Whitcombe Farm La
SHER DT9 11
Whitcross *RYEO* BA22 43
Whitehall Ct *CREWK* TA18 50
White Md *YEON* BA21 34
The Wilderness *SHER* DT9 39
Willey La *RYEO* BA22 22
Willow Farm *SHER* DT9 49
Willow Rd *YEON* BA21 2
Willow Tree Cl *RYEO* BA22 7
Wilton Rd *YEON* BA21 35
Winchester Gdns *YEON* BA21 35
Windermere Cl *YEOS* BA20 42
Windmill La *MCUTE* TA15 32
Windmill Ri *CREWK* TA18 50
Windsor La *SSH* TA14 31
Wine St *YEOS* BA20 3
Wingate Av *YEON* BA21 35
Wingfield Rd *SHER* DT9 38
Winston Dr *YEON* BA21 34
Winter La *SHER* DT9 18
Winyards Vw *CREWK* TA18 51
Wisteria Cl *RYEO* BA22 33
Woburn Rd *YEON* BA21 35
Woodcote *YEOS* BA20 42
Woodhenge *RYEO* BA22 33
Woodhouse La *MCUTE* TA15 32
RYEO BA22 17
Woodland Gv *YEOS* BA20 3
Woodland Ter *YEOS* * BA20 3
Woodstock Rd *YEON* BA21 35
Woollen La *RYEO* BA22 16
Wootton Gv *SHER* DT9 39
Wraxhill Rd *YEOS* BA20 42
Wydford Cl *SHER* DT9 38
Wyndham St *YEOS* BA20 3
Wyndham Vw *YEON* BA21 35
Wynnes Cl *SHER* DT9 38
Wynnes Ri *SHER* DT9 38
Wyvern Cl *YEOS* BA20 41

Y

Yarn Barton *YEOS* BA20 2
Yeo Va *RYEO* BA22 43
Yeovil Rd *CREWK* TA18 51
MCUTE TA15 32
RYEO BA22 22
SHER DT9 38
YEOS BA20 42
Yew Tree Cl *YEOS* BA20 42
York Pl *YEOS* BA20 3

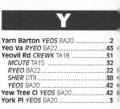

Index - featured places

Abbey Hill Trading Estate
YEON BA21 ....33 H3
All Saints CE Primary School
MCUTE TA15 ....32 A3
The Apples Medical Centre
SHER DT9 ....39 F3
Ashlands CE First School
CREWK TA18 ....50 C2
Barwick County Primary School
RYEO BA22 ....43 F4
Birchfield Primary School
YEON BA21 ....35 G2
Blacknell Industrial Estate
CREWK TA18 ....51 F4
Bucklers Mead Community School
YEON BA21 ....35 F1
Cadbury Business Park
RYEO BA22 ....5 E1
Cadbury Castle
RYEO BA22 ....11 G1
Castle Primary School
SSH TA14 ....30 D1
Chilthorne Domer CE Primary School
RYEO BA22 ....23 F4
Chilton Cantelo School
RYEO BA22 ....15 G2
Cineworld Yeovil
YEOS BA20 ....3 J5
Coldharbour Business Park
SHER DT9 ....39 E1
Coldharbour Hospital
SHER DT9 ....39 F1
Countess Gytha Primary School
RYEO BA22 ....9 H1
Crewkerne Health Centre
CREWK TA18 ....50 C4
Crewkerne Hospital
CREWK TA18 ....50 C4
Cropmead Trading Estate
CREWK TA18 ....51 E3
Fairmead School
YEON BA21 ....35 F1
Fiveways School
YEON BA21 ....35 G3
Fleet Air Arm Museum
RYEO BA22 ....7 H3
The George Shopping Centre
CREWK TA18 ....50 D3
Goldenstones Pool & Leisure Centre
YEOS BA20 ....3 F7
Grass Royal Junior School
YEON BA21 ....3 K2
Grove Medical Centre
SHER DT9 ....39 E2
The Gryphon School
SHER DT9 ....39 E1
Hamdon Medical Centre
SSH TA14 ....30 D2
Ham Hill Country Park
SSH TA14 ....31 F3
Hawkins Clinic
YEOS BA20 ....3 G5
Haynes Motor Museum
RYEO BA22 ....4 C2
Hazelgrove Kings Bruton Preparatory School
RYEO BA22 ....4 A3
Higher Farm Trading Estate
YEOS BA20 ....33 H4
Highfield Trading Estate
YEON BA21 ....3 K1
Holy Trinity CE Primary School
YEOS BA20 ....42 A1
Houndstone Business Park
RYEO BA22 ....33 G3
Houndstone Retail Park
RYEO BA22 ....33 G4
Huish Primary School
YEOS BA20 ....2 E4
Hundred Stone
YEON BA21 ....35 E1
Ilchester Community School (Infant)
RYEO BA22 ....6 B4
Ilchester Community School (Junior)
RYEO BA22 6
International College Sherborne School
SHER DT9 38
Ivel Barbarians RUFC
YEOS BA20 43
Job Centre
YEOS BA20 3
Johnson Hall & Octagon Theatre
YEOS BA20 3
Long Hazel International Caravan/Camping Park
RYEO BA22 4
Lufton Manor College
RYEO BA22 33
Lufton Trading Estate
RYEO BA22 33
Maiden Beech Community Middle School
CREWK TA18 50
Marksview Business Centre
YEON BA21 36
Martock Business Centre
MRTK TA12 20
Martock Business Park
MRTK TA12 20
Martock CE Primary School
MRTK TA12 20

ford J & I School
  YEON BA21 .... **35** E2
I Lane Trading Estate
  YEOS BA20 .... **3** H6
ntacute House
  MCUTE TA15 .... **32** A2
orlands Park
  Shopping Centre
  MRTK TA12 .... **20** B3
seum of South Somerset
  YEOS BA20 .... **3** F5
rth Cadbury CE
  Primary School
  RYEO BA22 .... **5** H1
rth Street Trading Estate
  CREWK TA18 .... **50** C2
rton Sub-Hamdon CE
  Primary School
  SSH TA14 .... **30** D4
rcroft Junior School
  YEOS BA20 .... **2** C4
e Park School
  YEOS BA20 .... **3** F3
n Mill Infant School
  YEON BA21 .... **35** G3
n Mill Trading Estate
  YEON BA21 .... **35** H3
nn House Day Hospital
  YEOS BA20 .... **3** G6
eston CE Primary School
  YEON BA21 .... **34** A4
eston Community School
  YEON BA21 .... **34** A4
eston Grove Medical Centre
  YEOS BA20 .... **2** C4
eston Road Clinic
  YEON BA21 .... **2** E2

The Quedam Shopping Centre
  YEOS BA20 .... **3** H4
Queen Camel Health Centre
  RYEO BA22 .... **10** A2
Reckleford Infant & School
  YEON BA21 .... **3** J3
RNAS Yeovilton
  RYEO BA22 .... **7** G4
St Andrews CE Primary School
  SHER DT9 .... **48** D4
St Bartholomews CE
  First School
  CREWK TA18 .... **51** E4
St Gildas RCVA Primary School
  YEON BA21 .... **3** H3
St Margarets CE Primary School
  RYEO BA22 .... **22** B3
St Martins Independent School
  CREWK TA18 .... **50** C3
St Mary's CE VC
  Primary School
  SHER DT9 .... **44** B3
Sherborne Abbey
  SHER DT9 .... **39** E4
Sherborne Abbey CE
  Primary School
  SHER DT9 .... **46** B1
Sherborne Castle
  SHER DT9 .... **39** G4
Sherborne FC
  SHER DT9 .... **39** F5
Sherborne Golf Club
  SHER DT9 .... **28** D3
Sherborne Museum
  SHER DT9 .... **39** E4
Sherborne Old Castle
  SHER DT9 .... **39** G3

Sherborne Police Station
  SHER DT9 .... **39** E4
Sherborne Preparatory School
  SHER DT9 .... **39** E4
Sherborne Primary School
  SHER DT9 .... **39** E2
Sherborne School
  SHER DT9 .... **39** E3
Sherborne School for Girls
  SHER DT9 .... **38** D3
Ski Centre
  YEOS BA20 .... **3** J6
South Western Business Park
  SHER DT9 .... **38** D4
Stanchester Community School
  SSH TA14 .... **31** G1
Stoke Sub Hamdon Priory
  SSH TA14 .... **30** D2
Swan Theatre
  SHER DT9 .... **3** G6
Swimming Pool
  SHER DT9 .... **44** C3
Thornford CE
  Primary School
  SHER DT9 .... **45** F5
Tintinhull House (NT)
  RYEO BA22 .... **22** B2
Wadham Community School
  CREWK TA18 .... **51** E2
West Coker Primary School
  RYEO BA22 .... **40** D5
Westfield Community School
  YEON BA21 .... **2** B1
Westfield Infants
  Community School
  YEON BA21 .... **2** B1
Yeatman Hospital
  SHER DT9 .... **39** E3

Yeo Leisure Park
  YEOS BA20 .... **3** J5
Yeovil Aerodrome
  YEOS BA20 .... **2** A5
Yeovil Athletic Arena
  YEON BA21 .... **34** D2
Yeovil Bowls & Squash Club
  YEON BA21 .... **3** F3
Yeovil Business Centre
  YEON BA21 .... **36** A3
Yeovil Bus Station
  YEOS BA20 .... **3** J5
Yeovil College
  YEON BA21 .... **3** F2
Yeovil College School of Art
  YEOS BA20 .... **2** D3
Yeovil Crematorium
  RYEO BA22 .... **33** G4
Yeovil District Hospital
  YEOS BA20 .... **3** G3
Yeovil Golf Club
  YEON BA21 .... **35** H5
Yeovil Showground
  YEOS BA20 .... **42** D3
Yeovil Small Business Centre
  RYEO BA22 .... **33** G3
Yeovil Town FC
  RYEO BA22 .... **33** G2
Youngs Endowed
  Primary School
  SHER DT9 .... **26** D4

Street by Street QUESTIONNAIRE

Dear Atlas User
Your comments, opinions and recommendations are very important to us.
So please help us to improve our street atlases by taking a few minutes
to complete this simple questionnaire.

You do NOT need a stamp (unless posted outside the UK). If you do not want to remove
this page from your street atlas, then photocopy it or write your answers on a plain sheet
of paper.

Send to: The Editor, AA Street by Street, FREEPOST SCE 4598,
Basingstoke RG21 4GY

ABOUT THE ATLAS...

Which city/town/county did you buy?

Are there any features of the atlas or mapping that you find particularly useful?

Is there anything we could have done better?

Why did you choose an AA Street by Street atlas?

Did it meet your expectations?

Exceeded ☐   **Met all** ☐   **Met most** ☐   **Fell below** ☐

Please give your reasons

Where did you buy it?

For what purpose? (please tick all applicable)

To use in your own local area ☐   To use on business or at work ☐

Visiting a strange place ☐   In the car ☐   On foot ☐

Other (please state)

LOCAL KNOWLEDGE...

Local knowledge is invaluable. Whilst every attempt has been made to make the information contained in this atlas as accurate as possible, should you notice any inaccuracies, please detail them below (if necessary, use a blank piece of paper) or e-mail us at *streetbystreet@theAA.com*

ABOUT YOU...

Name (Mr/Mrs/Ms)

Address

Postcode

Daytime tel no

E-mail address

Which age group are you in?

Under 25 ☐   25-34 ☐   35-44 ☐   45-54 ☐   55-64 ☐   65+ ☐

Are you an AA member?   YES ☐   NO ☐

Do you have Internet access?   YES ☐   NO ☐

Thank you for taking the time to complete this questionnaire. Please send it to us as soon as possible, and remember, you do not need a stamp (unless posted outside the UK).

We may use information we hold about you to write (email) or telephone you about other products and services offered by us and our carefully selected partners. Information may be disclosed to other companies in the Centrica group (including those using British Gas, Scottish Gas, Goldfish, One-Tel and AA brands) but we can assure you that we will not disclose it to third parties.

Please tick the box if you do NOT wish to recieve details of other products and services from the AA ☐

ML